The Good Soldier Sam

*Memoirs of an
East End Everyman*

Sam Berkovitz and Simon Blumenfeld

All Rights Reserved

No part of this book may be reproduced, stored in a retrieval system, or transmitted, in any form or by any means, electronic, mechanical, photocopying, recording or otherwise without prior permission of the copyright owner.

The Authors assert their moral right to be identified as the authors of this work.

First Published 2019

The Good Soldier Sam

ISBN: 9781798110454

Copyright © Sam Berkovitz and Simon Blumenfeld 2019

Foreword

This is the story of an everyman of his time, Sam Berkovitz. Born in London in 1905 of Jewish immigrants from Romania, Sam left school aged 14 following the death of his father. Spending his working life as a trousers cutter in the East End of London, he was self–educated, politically active, always curious about the wider world and had the advantage, or otherwise, of living in eventful times. This book recounts his life and that of ordinary people in East London during the first half of the 20th Century. It includes rent strikes, Mosley's attempted march through Cable Street, and the Spanish Civil War. Sam spent 3 years in the United States, timing his arrival perfectly to coincide with the Great Depression and its terrible consequences. Like many of his generation, he was an active member of the Communist Party, which at the time was seen to be the most authentic and effective vehicle for social and political change. Fearless in voicing his criticism, he became disillusioned with the Party at the time of the Jewish doctors' plot. Not one to shirk responsibility, although over-age and partially sighted, he succeeded in volunteering for active service in the Second World War, where he spent three and a half years in India and Burma and vividly relates the appalling fighting conditions.

By the time Sam decided in the 1980s to record his memoirs, he was blind: in addition, he had no experience of writing. However, his oldest and closest friend, Simon Blumenfeld, was a well-known novelist and journalist who, in the 1930s, had written about the East End and its people, and felt that Sam's story was well worth telling. For many months Simon would visit Sam's flat in Cannon Street Road, Stepney on a Sunday afternoon and, armed with a Dictaphone, record his story. Simon then had the task of transcribing the facts in his eloquent style, so that Sam, his acquaintances, his times and events sprung evocatively to life. Sam died in 1998 aged 92 and Simon in 2005 aged 97. This book is published as a tribute to them both.

Dr Barry Kenneth Bradbury Berkovitz 2019

Contents

Part 1 – Life in the East End   1

Sam describes the poverty of life in the East End at the turn of the twentieth century, having to leave school after the early death of his father and find work as a trousers cutter, his gambling on horses, and the necessity of the pawn shops.

Part 2 – America   31

Travelling to America twice as a young man and timing his second visit to coincide with the start of the Great Depression. Despite the terrible conditions that wiped out families and fortunes, his love affair with the country shines through.

Part 3 – Back In The East End   77

The international events affecting Sam's life in the 1930s, including Mosley's fascists, the Spanish civil war and the role of the Communist Party in these events.

Part 4 – The War   91

Despite being partially sighted and over-age, Sam succeeds in volunteering for active service. After a period of training in England, he spends more than three years in India and Burma. The appalling conditions of fighting are described, though with more deaths through diseases than in combat. He recalls his training with the Chindits and his platoon being addressed by the charismatic figure of Major-General Orde Wingate. Ironically, having been promoted and unfairly demoted, he enters and leaves the armed forces as a Private.

Part 5 – Back Home   171

Sam returns back from the war lucky to have survived. He recounts his struggles to earn a living in post-war east London, the rent strikes and his eventual split from the Communist Party. His degenerating eyesight worsens and his total blindness eventually forces him into retirement.

Simon Blumenfeld

Simon Blumenfeld was unique in several fields: in revolutionary politics, as a novelist, playwright and journalist. In his 20s and 30s, he published four novels, of which the best known is the influential 'Jew Boy', presenting him as a keen documenter of the Jewish East End. Largely self-educated and an active Marxist, he was involved in organising volunteers for the Spanish Civil War and against Mosley. He became a correspondent for a French news agency, simultaneously turning out cowboy novels under the pseudonym of Huck Messer, from the Yiddish meaning 'hand chopper'. During World War II, Simon became a script-writer for Stars In Battledress, an army talent show, which was his entrée into the world of show business. As a prolific journalist, Simon became the light entertainment editor of 'The Stage'. His 40 years working for that influential magazine provided him with an extraordinary breadth of showbiz friends and acquaintances, including Paul Robeson, Mistinguette, the Beatles and Barbara Windsor among many others. He entered the Guinness Book of Records as the world's oldest columnist at 97, shortly before he died.

Part 1

Life in the East End

Chapter 1

I cut the trouser fronts and then turned the cloth to get the backs done. I put my scissors down and suddenly found I couldn't see it. I was groping for it and couldn't find it. It was a fourteen-inch long gunmetal scissors; the table was light so it should have stood out a mile, but I searched for it and just couldn't see it.

The guv'nor, standing opposite, noticed me groping for the scissors.

He said, "What's the matter, Sam?"

I said, "I can't find the blooming scissors" and he said, "It's right there. Right under your bloody nose!"

I couldn't laugh that away. It was obvious that my eyes were a darned sight worse than I'd ever imagined. I'd known my vision was bad for a long time; now he knew, and I knew he knew. I'd really had it. There was no point in putting it off any longer, so right there and then I decided to call it a day. "Julian," I told him, "Come the holidays in a couple of weeks, I'm going to retire. I'm causing far too many hold-ups here."

Over the past few years while working for Julian I'd set the machinists more and more problems. When I cut out checkered materials, for example, they found the patterns didn't always match because I had confused the shades. The girls were literally carrying me. They never complained. They were all friends of mine and were only too pleased to sort things out except that now, increasingly, they couldn't be sorted out satisfactorily.

I'd come to a full stop. Not because I wanted to, I was 68, already three years beyond pensionable age, but still in good shape physically. I could have gone on to 70 or longer without any bother. I wasn't averse to work. I didn't mind working although I'd always hated the workshop, and I didn't mind stopping. My attitude was that I was willing to do it for as long as I could. Now I couldn't.

Period. And that was an end to it.

Prodded by my wife, I went to Moorfields Eye Hospital for a check-up. They told me my condition was irreversible. The sight of one eye was very bad and the other was suffering from degeneration of the retina and would only get worse. The best thing they could recommend was carrying a white stick to warn people I was blind.

After drawing my pension for a couple of weeks and doing nothing else, I began to feel restless. Hearing about part-time jobs a lot of local men my age were getting – the City must have been full of retired tailors running errands – I went to an agency. Naturally, I hid my white stick, and they sent me up to Kingsway in the West End for a job with a firm of patent lawyers and engineers, where I was given a nice little cubbyhole. I sat there until wanted after the mail was sorted, and ran errands, mainly delivering messages to offices in the vicinity.

For me this was a piece of cake. It was my old shop boy routine updated, only I was now carrying envelopes instead of wrappers bulging with made-up trousers.

From my earliest youth I was cut out to be a shop boy. I had a talent for it. Even in my prime when I was living in New York and working as a skilled trousers cutter, I enjoyed doing the workshop errands around Canal Street. A reluctant tailor, I gladly accepted any excuse for leaving the workshop and wandering about the city.

Being a London shop boy in the early years of the century was a calling never acknowledged by the Ministry of Labour. Officially we didn't exist, but every workshop had at least one, and many had two or more kids of nine or ten, like me and even younger. We started work after school hours. We'd hurry home at four, grab a hunk of bread and jam and rush to the workshop, in my case the room next door where my father struggled to make a living.

When I left with my wrapper of completed garments, I was as bright as a bird, especially Saturday when I started early, around eight o'clock in the morning and was on my rounds all day till the shops closed at seven. During the slack season there was nothing at all doing Monday, Tuesday and Wednesday. We'd go to the shops with empty wrappers and return with empty wrappers. A little work, however, usually came in for the weekend. If there was a rush for funeral or wedding specials, I'd collect the raw materials and trimmings on Saturday morning and deliver the completed trousers straight after school on Monday, even though it meant people in the workshop slogging away all Saturday and Sunday and sometimes through the night.

We shop boys were a bright bunch of kids. We had to be because we were entrusted with valuable garments to collect and deliver and had to find our way all over London on our own. We met at crossroads in the City and in the cutting rooms of merchant tailors' establishments and bespoke houses in the suburbs, and by the time we were teenagers we were quite men of the world.

My particular friend was Harry Taylor, a roly-poly youngster who had a brain like a computer and could work out odds quicker than any adult bookie. At 13 he matriculated, but all this brilliance didn't help him much; he ended up like the majority of us bright boys, in the workshop.

Our careers in the world of industry developed in three stages. Stage one was running errands as shop boys from the ages of nine or ten. Stage two was the tailor's workshop where you started to learn the trade when you left school at 14 – to the very day - no nonsense about waiting till the end of term. Then, as you got older and graduated to journeyman status entitling you to draw an adult wage, you entered stage three, which meant going straight on the dole where you stayed on and off, mostly on, for the rest of your working life.

After we left school I didn't see much of Harry, but I bumped into him some years later outside the Labour Exchange.

"Got any money, Sam?" he asked me.

"Not a light. – You?"

"Broke to the wide," he said. He pulled his trouser pockets inside out to show me. "I've even hocked my last waistcoat," he added.

"What do you mean 'hocked your last waistcoat?' A waistcoat?"

"That's right. A waistcoat," he said. "You may not believe this, Sam, but a waistcoat is worth two shillings and ten pence at our friendly neighbourhood pawnbroker, less fourpence ha'penny of course, for the ticket."

I was astonished. "You mean that?"

He nodded. "Of course I mean it."

"Well, why didn't somebody tell me this before? – I've got three new waistcoats hanging up. Since I've been to the States I'm strictly a two-piece man, jacket and pants only."

"So what are we waiting for?" Harry enquired politely. We chased around to my lodgings. I got the waistcoats and we went to pay a business call on Mr Dicker in Sidney Street. He welcomed us with open arms, and with no arguing the toss about the price, forked out three times two shillings and ten pence, less four pence for the ticket. He was a peculiar, wizened, little character, this Mr Dicker, like someone out of Dickens. He was always 'Mr Dicker' to his face but usually 'Uncle' between ourselves. He still dried the ink on the tickets with fine sand and wrote them out three at a time with an outsize penholder which had three nibs attached. One ticket he gave me, another he pinned to the waistcoats and the third he placed in a large safe behind the counter.

What earthly use were waistcoats without jackets and pants, I wondered? Harry didn't know either. All he was fairly certain about was that, like every other unredeemed pledge, they were sold after a statutory period had elapsed.

In 1944 during the war, now Private Berkovitz. S. No. 13091795, I was on the march in India. Leaving Cawnpore *en route* for another large city, what should I see coming towards me on the road but a couple of Mr Dicker's unredeemed pledges! The waistcoats draped the torsos of two stalwart Pathans. Their traditional garb, thin white linen tunics and trousers having no pockets, and the Pathans being the shopkeepers, tallymen and moneylenders of central Northern India, the waistcoats were their business premises. They had poems in one pocket, receipts in another, small change in the third and notes and other documents in a fourth. Except for the grime and the dust, either of the waistcoats could have been mine. It was a lesson in elementary economics, underlining the interdependence of world trade with clothing as universally accepted currency.

In comparison with my early years as a shop boy, my latest Kingsway job was as near paradise as I could reasonably hope to get. I was doing the thing I liked and did best, walking the streets of London and getting paid for it, to boot. But inside two weeks it was paradise lost. My boss happened to look out of the window and became petrified watching me barge across Kingsway warding off the traffic with my white stick. He was very understanding about it, however. When I came back to the office he said, "Sam, you nearly gave me heart failure. Why didn't you tell me you were blind? I'm sorry, but I don't think I could be responsible for you."

I dredged up from memory a patriotic old Music Hall number and sang half a chorus: "You don't want to lose me, but you think I ought to go?"

My boss nodded. "I couldn't have put it better." He paid me off right away like a gentleman, giving me an extra week's wages in lieu.

I had started as a shop boy. I'd been at it for close on 60 years and at the end of my working career I finished up as a shop boy. That, in a nutshell, is the story of my life.

Chapter 2

I used to wake up sometimes in the middle of the night and wonder why I couldn't sleep. Then I'd remember. It was the noise of the traffic on the river. Now there isn't any. No traffic to speak of any more. No noise. The plaintive honks of ships entering the Pool of London, which used softly to punctuate the foggy nights, are silent. I can sit a whole morning in Shadwell Park, facing the river, and be lucky to hear the occasional freighter coming upstream to supply Battersea power station's fuel.

When I was a kid, the river in Stepney pulsated with life. You saw it, you felt it, you heard it and you smelt it. There was an endless procession of ships disgorging cargoes from all over the world. Their special presence flavoured the air with distinctive aromas: apples from Australia, pepper and spices from the Indies, tea from Ceylon (now Sri Lanka) and olives, cheeses and wines from the continent.

I have lived in the same flat for getting on for fifty years, a couple of hundred yards from the old St Katharine Docks, and I was born not a quarter of a mile away. The Thames has always fascinated me and drawn me like a lover. Even in my earliest days as a shop boy, my favourite itinerary was dominated by the river.

I loved going to Woolwich where my father made trousers for a shop in Beresford Square. There were several different ways of getting there. I could go via the South London Railway to New Cross and take the tram costing two pence all the way to Beresford Square; I could go from New Cross Gate, which was on the old London-Brighton line, and take a two-penny tram all the way, skirting the entire boundary of South East London where there were still farms in actual production. I was staggered the first time I saw a corn field in the London area flourishing almost in the shadow of Tower Bridge.

The way I liked to come home best, sacrificing the penny on the fare I could have saved and kept for myself by walking through Blackwall Tunnel, was to go down Hare Street to the Woolwich Ferry, cross over to North Woolwich and get a bus back all the way to Whitechapel. The journey led through causeways and cluttered dock areas thronged with masses of shipping. There were huge vessels, so large that the swing bridges had to be held up for them to pass through and I could literally lean over and touch them. In all my travels since, I have never come across so many merchantmen congregated together in any one place.

Summer time, I loved to loiter in the narrow alleyways threading inland from the riverside. Here too were special activities: gaunt old women, grey hair pulled back in tight, sparse buns behind grey faces, were at work in the street. They wore heavy sacking aprons and with legs akimbo they cradled in their laps coloured sails from the Thames barges, patching them up with needles thick as bodkins. Right there on the pavement they performed chores for the ships' chandlers lining the Highway, stitching and knotting in deep brown shadow like the dark Vincent of the Potato Eaters.

I don't pretend to be a paragon of virtue, yet I can claim the odds in my favour were always two to one. I was never a womaniser and I never drank to excess, but I must admit to a lifelong passion for gambling. It's understandable. Being born poor, a Jew in a Whitechapel slum when the twentieth century was just a few years old, was in itself a fearful hazard. In betting terms, staying alive at birth was probably less than a fifty-fifty shot. In my case it was further complicated by the fact that I was one of triplets. That raised the odds immeasurably against my survival. Come to think of it, I never met triplets my age who grew to maturity in the East End.

In those days, nobody went to hospital for anything so trivial as having babies. When the time came, my father was sent for a walk with my elder brother. Two of our neighbours, scrubbed arms bared to the elbows and surrounded by bleached linen cloths and borrowed basins filled with boiling water, installed themselves in the bedroom and took charge of the confinement.

There were three of us, apparently all stillborn, laid out on the kitchen table like pathetic little skinned rabbits. The women were attending to my mother, when I coughed. The older midwife rushed in at once, pounced on me and pummeled me into life. When I grew up, she used to grab me when I was playing in the street and show me off as a miracle to passing strangers. So, I coughed my way into life and I've had a slight cough ever since, though as I am now long past the allotted biblical span it doesn't seem to have done me much harm.

I suppose one could say my very first gamble had come up; for the rest of my life, however, in every game of chance I ventured, I have been a consistent loser. I did have a lot of little wins over the years - one's bound to by the law of averages - and also the occasional big win. Once I collected £200 in a single wager, which is probably worth ten times that much in modern monetary terms, but I never really hit the jackpot, except in the chanciest gamble of all, marriage, when I met Bessie Cohen and made her my wife.

A gambler is permanently short of money. He always, as they say, lacks two days to his year, so it's important for him to have a convenient source for obtaining a few shillings in a hurry. Fortunately, in the East End, three such legitimate channels were instantly available: bookies, ragmen and pawnbrokers. They all dealt in ready cash. From the bookies, money came through guessing long odds winners, and from the ragmen, via sacks full of woollen cuttings called 'mungo', plentiful only during the busy season. The pawnbrokers however, were fixed stars in our storm-tossed firmament. They always had money if you had something to hock. It soon became evident that my mission in life was to deplete the coffers of the third, the pawnbrokers, in order to augment those of the first, the bookies. Betting, I discovered, was a business open to life's losers. It was the only business where all you needed was a capital of a couple of shillings.

Pawnbrokers, like kids, were a dominant feature of the East End landscape. This inspired me to promulgate 'Berks' Law', which lays down that the number of pawn shops in any given area is inversely proportional to the incidence of birth control clinics. In our street, Bedford Street, later renamed Cavell Street in honour of Nurse Edith Cavell, the first world war heroine, there were always dozens of kids skylarking around on the pavements and in the roadway. On the other side of Commercial Road in the area of St George's, it was worse. The bottom of Cannon Street Road, Cable Street and The Highway were clogged with the weekend spawn of Irish dockers. On Sundays, it was Mass in the morning at St Mary and St Michael, then over to the Mann and Crossman pub in the afternoon and on to the missus in the evening. The results were affectionately known as 'Mann and Crossman tiddlers'.

Now, you're lucky to see half a dozen kids in Cavell Street, and you won't find a pawnbroker anywhere. Blind as I am, I can lead you to a score of betting shops within a hundred yards radius of my flat, but I couldn't direct you to a single pawnshop.

The same obtains to synagogues. The *shuls* were far more numerous in this part of Stepney than pawnbrokers. Sometimes, there were two or three in a single small street. There was even one right next door to where I live now. Today, this, and most of the other synagogues have vanished – along with the congregations.

Our Mr Dicker was a jewel among pawnbrokers. His was an ever-open maw. He ran his premises in Sidney Street like a high-class social club. The regulars in their separate pews peeked above the partitions and conversed amiably while awaiting their turn to be served. They were mostly housewives with bundles of laundry or their husbands' Sunday best.

The washing was clean and impeccably ironed. The women knew better than to try and deceive Mr Dicker. He had a set of sensitive probes grafted onto the tips of his fingers. They led him unerringly to holes and stains no matter how cunningly concealed. His customers only attempted to cheat him once. He would look at them reproachfully, reject the bundle and it was 'never again'. But when he knew them, he accepted their pledges without demur or examination, handed over the few shillings, and returned them unopened, usually at the weekend.

The years had bestowed on Mr Dicker a tremendous expertise over a wide range of artefacts. At a glance he knew to the last half-penny the value of a pair of scuffed shoes, some lace-edged pillow slips, petit-point embroidery, Georgian snuff boxes or an antique carriage clock purloined by some coachman grandfather in the service of a long dead country squire.

Mr Dicker was a tiny person. With his long frock coat greened with age, his half-moon spectacles, gleaming grey eyes peering above them and shining bald head, he looked like a displaced leprechaun. He was so small he had to stand on a podium to be visible over the counter. As an apprentice he had 'lived-in' above the shop. Now the manager, and a life-long bachelor, he ran the place with one assistant and 'lived-in' still, upstairs. The owner was an absentee landlord who had inherited Mr Dicker along with the shop and considerable slum property. A short, florid man who resided in some style in St John's Wood, he made an appearance in Sidney Street once a year for the annual stocktaking and was then not seen again for another twelve months.

In my late teens when I was living in a room in the East End, I used to hock my best suit every Monday morning and take it out on Friday when I had earned a few shillings. When I didn't show up on a Monday, the women would ask "Where's the long-un?" and one of them usually came up with the right answer: "He must have had a winner."

Mr Dicker used to treat everyone with the same old-fashioned courtesy. The scruffiest washerwoman was 'Madam' and he never failed to call me 'Sir'. When my suit, handed across the counter, looked a bit under the weather, he would chide me: "You have been very remiss with this garment, Sir." And he would show me once again how to brush it properly and hang it correctly.

Came the time when the suit was so woebegone that Mr Dicker wouldn't go to my usual twenty-five shillings. "I'm very sorry, Sir," he said firmly. "I can only offer you one pound" (twenty shillings). This threatened to dislocate my entire economic strategy. "But Mr Dicker," I protested. "I must have the twenty-five shillings. I need a pound of that to carry me through to the end of the week." "I am giving you a pound, Sir," he pointed out gently. I had to explain. "But I need the extra five shillings for a win double. I've got two horses that are an absolute cert." Mr Dicker was no *shmuk* when it came to horses, either. He adjusted his spectacles and leaned over the counter. "Which two horses did you have in mind?" I unfurled my Sporting Life, shoved it beneath his nose and showed him my underscored selections. The shrewd grey eyes looked down at the 'pink un' and then up at me and he slowly shook his head. "I can't possibly give you the other five shillings, Sir," he said. "Not for these two no-hopers. Believe me, you'll thank me when you come to redeem your pledge. Now Sir, is it to be a pound?"

Once Mr Dicker had made up his mind, nothing could shake him. He was right, of course. They were both also rans. But I didn't tell him when I took out my suit that I had half-starved myself and backed them. Dicker being Mr Dicker, however, probably guessed. Taking him all in all, he was a true friend of the working classes.

Chapter 3

I was over 60 when I started work for Julian. My idea of heaven was now shaping, like a Highland malt at my elbow, Mozart's music in my ears and a racing form book on the table. The wanderlust was fading fast and the lure of America so diminished, I'd happily settle for one more trip to the West Coast, this time to San Francisco. I really wanted to see that town after all I had read about it in Jack London's books. Then I'd call it a day.

There wasn't an earthly chance of saving enough money from my wages for the trip. But there was always my old tempter, the bookie. As I got older my wages got smaller, so the odds had to be larger. Time was not on my side: it had to be a big win now, or San Francisco never. Everyone in Julian's workshop gambled, even the shop boys. It's a way of life still in the East End: you don't amass big money by the sweat of your brow; you either steal it or win it.

Our machinist, a comfortably-built forty-ish woman named Rosie, had a good record for picking the odd winner. She came up to me one morning during the tea break and said "Sam, you want to go to San Francisco?" I said, "Rosie, you know I do. Any suggestions?" As a fellow punter she was privy to my dreams of affluence. "Two," she said. "Both horses. If you back them," she said, "I'll guarantee you a trip to San Francisco and your return fare with money to spare."

My first impulse was to laugh at her. When she gave me her selections I laughed still more. I produced my scratch sheet and showed her their form, both studded with long strings of *bagels* – zeros in racing parlance. Being an experienced racehorse speculator, having lost consistently for close on half a century, I considered their possibilities and dismissed them out of hand. I concluded my analysis with an expert flourish of certainty. "They'll never win in a million years," I pronounced. "If they do you can kick me."

Next morning she came in and kicked me. Hard. If I'd been a contortionist I'd have repeated the operation myself. Harder. They'd won at 20 to 1 and 33 to 1 respectively. A pound double would have netted me £713 and that trip to San Francisco.

Rosie herself had put two shillings on the horses and drew a tidy sum. It wasn't blind chance that pointed Rosie in that direction. It was positively an instruction from higher authority. Only the previous week Rosie and her husband had been appearing as character witnesses at the Old Bailey. It was in defence of their son, who was being tried on a serious charge – holding up a security van. Their impassioned pleas moved the judge, before he sent junior away for a good long stretch, to call the father a "fine old gentleman" and tell Rosie: "I have to consider the safety and security of the public, although your plea in court touches me."

The names of the horses were 'Plea in Court' and 'Fine Old Gentleman'. Their utterly fortuitous pairing made what we gamblers call - nobody seems to know why - a busman's double – probably because you usually have to wait forever for one, and then two to turn up. Personally, I don't regard gambling as a gamble, but a form of investment. In view of the long odds and the big prizes, obviously it has to be highly speculative, but to me it's no different from investing on the Stock Exchange where it is just as easy to lose your money.

On occasions, gambling has been a real life-saver. Forty-odd years ago, Lou Berman came to me with a problem. It was Wednesday and he was due to get married the following Monday, August Bank Holiday. For a year Lou and his fiancée had been pooling their bits of cash to get a little flat together. Now there were only a few more days to go and they still didn't have enough money to move in and take possession.

"How much money do you need?" I asked him. "Twenty-five pounds," he said.

I was working full-time; there was the wife and my baby son and all I was earning was three pounds and ten shillings a week, with an occasional extra for a cutting job on the side. I whistled. "No good asking me. I don't know where you'd get that kind of money. If I stood up in the street and auctioned myself off I couldn't get twenty-five pounds." Lou was dejected. It was the truth. I tried to cheer him up. "I'll tell you what. I fancy two horses tomorrow. If you can risk ten shillings I'll risk ten shillings and we can just about make it if we're lucky."

Lou knew the usual fate of my fancies but he had reached the might-as-well-be-hanged-for-a-sheep stage. He agreed, shrugged his shoulders and gave me the money. "With or without that ten shillings I'm in dead trouble anyway," he said. So, I made a double. I still remember the horses – 'Sole Exit' and 'Mendicant Friar'. Sole Exit won at around 10 to 1 and Mendicant Friar romped home at 7 to 2. The bookie paid me forty-one pounds, eighteen shillings and nine pence, more than enough to give Lou the twenty-five pounds he needed. When I gave Lou the money, his face lit up and I felt like Santa Claus. I thought, in what other way could I possibly have got twenty-five pounds for him and on top of that a considerable sum for myself?

Since then, I've been hooked on the horses but, as a responsible married man, I've kept a grip on my gambling. I only lose what I can afford to and, on the rare occasion when a win comes up, the wife and I have a little ball.

Of course, I don't always gamble. I've often gone a couple of days without a bet. Not like a friend of mine, Yossul, who, in those early thirties was involved in gambling of some sort every waking moment. He was the type of character described in the magistrates' court as 'of no fixed abode,' which wasn't strictly true, because Yossul had half-a-dozen fixed abodes, usually in one of the local billiard halls. He frequently dossed down in Sunshine's Club, which was open all night. He slept on whatever was available, an old sofa, or one of the tattier tables that stood untenanted in the corner covered by a thick rubberised sheet. He paid for his 'kip' by an occasional half-hearted sortie round the floor in the daytime, sweeping up cigarette ends.

Yossul was born Joseph Levy. He was tiny, dark, wiry and agile, with bulging pop-eyes. Everybody called him Yossul or referred to him by his alias, 'The Kid from Spain', after the Eddie Cantor movie of the same name. He was as honest as the day – fatal for a gambler. He might not have a penny of his own in his pocket but held stakes of quite considerable amounts. He was sent to buy fresh packs of cards, to shuffle them and, when the boys were feeling particularly charitable, even allowed to deal. He set up the snooker balls on their correct spots, marked scores, handed over cue rests and called time when the hour was up. If he wasn't continually in an ambience of *spielers* (gamblers), Yossul wasn't alive. This *schlemiel* (fool) suddenly got lucky. It happens to everyone, once. He must have been in his late twenties, older by some years than the rest of us, but when he collected a hundred and fifty pounds from the bookie he spread the notes on a shaky card table in Sunshine's and looked at them with glazed eyes like a scared kid, still not believing they actually belonged to him.

We – about half a dozen of us – decided to take Yossul in hand. "You're going to start living like a *mensch*" (gentleman), we told him, "and look decent for once in your life."

We engaged a furnished back room for him at ten shillings a week and paid a month's rent in advance. This was to break him in gently again to the basic desiderata of civilized behaviour. Then we took him to the best bespoke tailor in Whitechapel, chose the material and ordered a made-to-measure suit of the finest worsted and a handsome pure wool Crombie overcoat also tailored to our specification. We paid for them on the spot in cash before a single stitch was inserted in either. We knew our Yossul. He could quite easily call the whole thing off if he was running short and needed money. We bought a dozen good shirts, ties, several pairs of shoes, socks and a hat, and gave Yossul the change - £25.

At that time, a suit or overcoat took about two weeks to complete with two fittings for a made-to-measure suit or overcoat. Long before then Yossul's £25 had gone. He had disappeared from Sunshine's for a start and was now hanging round a better class gambling joint in Bishopsgate. As he couldn't wear his smart accessories without his new suit and coat, he took hat, shirts, ties and shoes into the obliging Mr Dicker and pawned the lot. By the time he collected his suit and overcoat that money had gone too, so those garments went straight from the tailor's workshop into the stockroom of our saviour of Sidney Street.

By the end of the following week, Yossul was hawking at 3 or 4 shillings a time, or for anything he could get, the pawn tickets of his entire wardrobe and happily sleeping once again, broke, on the old billiard table in Sunshine's.

Chapter 4

Mickey Shitbags (ne Michael Goldstein) ran his own little club not far from Sunshine's. Like Sunshine's, Mickey's had a quality shared with all the upper-crust West End clubs – it was a strictly masculine enclave. No women were allowed within those sacred portals – even the odd cleaner was some broken down old pug or a gambler on his beam ends.

Mickey's club consisted of a couple of billiard tables, a small bar for sandwiches and teas, some rickety card tables, a few kitchen chairs and a telephone. The phone was important, certainly the most important fixture on the premises, because it was Shitbags' real business as private betting was illegal. The club was only a front for his activities as a bookie, and most of his time during racing hours was spent with his lips glued to the mouthpiece relaying bets to the office.

Where or how he earned his soubriquet 'Shitbags' was debatable, but there were two obvious possibilities. One was his mean, penny-pinching attitude towards his fellow men; the other an oblique reference to his baggy trousers belted round his sagging paunch with an old tie and drooping in loose folds between his crotch, like a Balkan peasant's diarrhoea drawers.

I came in the club one afternoon to place a bet for the last race. I was playing a whole pound because it had been passed on to me as a hot tip by some very special 'inside information'. Mickey took my pound and went to the phone but there was either pressure of business at the other end or a fault on the line: he couldn't get through till past post-time. Reluctantly, he handed back my money: "Sorry Sam," he said. "I can't get it on." "Look Mickey," I protested. "It's only 6 to 1. At most 7! Cover the bet yourself."

"Sorry Sam," he repeated. "You know I don't take bets. I pass them on to the office and they pay me commission."

"But it's only six quid," I said. "Even if you lose. Maybe seven. I've taken chances on bets like that myself a dozen times, though I'm only a common old working man."

"That's as may be," said Mickey. "That's why you're only a common old working man, and I've got my own club. Because I don't take chances. I work only on percentages, strictly by the book." Actually, I wasn't surprised. That was Mickey Shitbags. Six or seven pounds was really nothing to someone in his line of business, who could lay his hands on hundreds of pounds whenever he wanted it. He simply couldn't be bothered to do anybody a good turn, even when there was only the slightest risk attached.

It so happened that my inside information wasn't all that on the nose; the horse came fifth. For days after, Mickey posed as a public benefactor, telling anyone who bothered to listen that he had saved me from insolvency by refusing to accept my life savings on a nag he knew to be a *stummer* (useless).

A week or so later Mickey slouched over to me in the club, reeking more than usual of tobacco and whisky and, with a grandiloquent gesture, he shoved my five shilling bet in his pocket and without making a beeline for the phone, said "You're on." "How come?" I said. "Taking the bet yourself? It's 10 to 1 – could cost you all of fifty shillings!" Mickey sneered. "A 10 to 1 shot's got as much chance of winning that race as a man landing on the moon! That's the trouble with all you *schnorrers*," (beggars) he said. "You're always looking for long odds. That's why you're *schnorrers* and you'll always stay that way. The wise guy goes along with the big money. The odds don't count. It's the safe return that matters." He leaned forward confidentially. "I'll tell you something. For days the money's been flooding in on 'Mumtaz Mahal'. Big money. That's where mine's going. Not peanuts either. On the Aga Khan's Mumtaz Mahal."

"You must be crazy," I said. "It's 5 to 1 on."

"Less than that," said Mickey. "It's a 100 to 8. I've put £500 on Mumtaz Mahal to win forty pounds. That's the way someone with a genuine knowledge of the turf operates. He doesn't fling his money around like you *schnorrers,* making ten shilling bets scratching for long odds for accumulators. He waits. He bides his time, then he lays centuries on certainties."

Well, in this instance, there couldn't possibly be a bigger racing certainty. Only two horses on a five-furlong dash and one of them

Mumtaz Mahal, with champion jockey Gordon Richards riding it. Mumtaz Mahal, as sweet a filly as ever munched oats, the fastest thing on four legs and never beaten once in a dozen outings. Mickey didn't have to rub it in. It was indeed money for old rope. But you needed money first to take advantage of the situation. What would be the percentage laying out my usual two shillings to win two pence?

In those days, there were no gates on the course and 'under starters orders' took horses' noses to the tape. At the off Mumtaz Mahal reared and Gordon Richards, the greatest jockey in Britain, maybe in the whole world, fell off. The other runner, a nothing horse, a selling-plater by comparison, ambled over the distance and was past the post before a shaken Gordon Richards could put himself to rights. For a couple of days Mickey's shop didn't open. He'd been ill, he said, when he appeared again. More likely he was tired of taking it out on his wife, who was often seen in the street sporting black eyes when Mickey had been at the malt too often.

For weeks afterwards, Mickey was the complete misanthrope. He loomed over us unexpectedly while we were laughing among ourselves during an innocent game of cards. His liquor and cigar-sodden breath wafted right over the shuffled decks. "What's so funny, eh?" he would demand suspiciously. Then he would turn his back on us and walk away quickly before anyone had a chance to reply.

Mumtaz Mahal means 'the distinguished one of the palace.' It bore reference to the favourite wife of the Mogul emperor Shah Jahan. When she died, crushed, it was said, by an elephant, he was inconsolable and built a marble mausoleum in her memory called the Taj Mahal. During the Second World War when I was stationed for a while in Agra, I could see the white tips of the minarets gleaming in the distance, but I never once went to visit it. That wasn't a bit like me. Usually I made a beeline for any local artefact of historical interest. I only had to see a picture of an ancient Buddha in my vicinity and on my first free day I was there, but for some absurd reason I can't even remember now, time and time again I kept putting off a trip to the Taj Mahal, until movement orders caught up with me and it was too late. Now I shall never see the Taj Mahal in all its glory, even if I win the pools and get to Agra again.

Still on the topic of India, on my first day in Rawalpindi, I saw a sheet of paper pinned to the notice board of our company office with details of a monument to Alexander the Great. This huge stone mound I never saw either, but this time it wasn't my fault. I made several serious attempts to get there, but was foiled by unexpected fatigues and sudden changes of routine, until when I had finally perfected a foolproof itinerary, sadly the order came to pack up and leave. The whole area between Rawalpindi and Lahore was full of associations with Alexander the Great.

We were still using roads he had built to supply his foot soldiers thousands of years before. Alexander the Great was unquestionably a military genius. He must have been a gambling man too. No-one but a gambler would have risked taking a small army and setting out to conquer the entire known world. What's more he succeeded against almost impossible odds, and no soldier before or since has equalled his feats in the field.

I was really sorry to leave Rawalpindi without visiting the Alexander monument. It seemed as if I was missing something not only spectacular, but important, and only recently I discovered what it was. The monument was not to Alexander, but was erected by him to commemorate his horse, Bucephalus. Anyone who can put up a monument to his horse is a man after my own heart.

Chapter 5

My father was one of that select band of *fusgayers* – literally foot travellers – who in the '80s and '90s shook the inhospitable dust of their native Rumania from their boots and took the long overland trek to Hamburg and then a boat to England. Some 2,903 Rumanian *fusgayers* eventually arrived in London and of these, 375 travelled on to America. Of the remainder, the Jewish Board of Guardians, hard-pressed to support their own paupers, promptly returned 1,399 to their country of origin reluctantly adding 1,129 new *schnorrers* to their books.

My father was one of the fortunate 1,129, but he had no need of charity from the Board of Guardians or anyone else. A skilled tailor, he got a job inside a week with a *landsman* from a previous intake who was now established in his own workshop as a trousers maker.

Settled in lodgings, he joined a little Rumanian synagogue in Fieldgate Street. There were dozens of such old-home-orientated *shuls* (synagogues) in Stepney to serve the needs of immigrants anxious to meet *landsleit* (landsmen) from back home (*der heim*) while they accustomed themselves to living in a strange milieu. Through friends in the synagogue he met my newly-arrived mother and they were married at the turn of the century.

My father had no relatives in Britain. His younger sister Soorah died in America and he had last seen his eldest sister Bayleh in Bucharest, where she had some sort of shadowy job in an *haute couture* house. Bayleh was an adventurous lady in every sense. Before the First World War, we got a card from Buenos Aires signed Bella. After the war, we heard from her (another card, from California) signed Beulah. Then, in the summer of 1919 she was with us in person - Mrs Bettina Morrison, the wife of a Scots superintendent of police in the Straits Settlement, a group of British territories located in Southeast Asia.

I found her the most beautiful creature alive. I had only seen people like Aunt Bettina before on the silent screen in the Palaseum, our local fleapit in the Commercial Road. She looked like Nazimova with her dark shining eyes, tufts of puffed hair struggling out of the cloche hat she had pressed down over one eye, a big black beauty spot just above her chin, square shoulders, nipped-in waist jacket and long flared skirt revealing a flash of white ribbed stockings above a sleek, high-heeled lace-up black boot. She wouldn't hear of any objections to taking the whole lot of us down to Cliftonville for a week's holiday in the resort's sole kosher boarding house. Luckily it was the slack season, so my father was only too glad to close up his workshop.

The only one left behind was grandmother, *die booba*, my mother's mother, a formidable old lady, always dressed in sombre garments, with a black, head-shawl like a Greek widow. She resolutely refused to leave the East End under any pretext and viewed everything English with unquenchable disapproval. To the end of her days, *die booba* never moved alone beyond the periphery of Tower Hamlets. She never spoke anything but Rumanian and Yiddish, which was really no inconvenience as everybody else in Bedford Street spoke Yiddish, even the occasional patrolling policeman. She religiously read Moshe Myers' *'Die Zeit'* every day, went once a week to the Yiddish Theatre at the Pavilion and read all the Yiddish romances recommended by Mr Bogdan in the Whitechapel library.

I still remember that full week's holiday, because the next one I had was on my honeymoon nearly twenty years later. As for Aunt Bettina, she vanished as suddenly as she came, and we never heard from her again – not even a postcard.

Mother more than made up for the lack of family on my father's side. Her brothers and sisters – my aunts, uncles and cousins- proliferated in all directions. They oozed from every East End nook and cranny. It was something to see and hear when they gathered at a relative's house for a party (*a simcha*) and Rumanians never needed much excuse for a celebration. They were all short and squat, unlike my father who was exceptionally tall and rather slim. The women stayed in the kitchen and talked babies and winter clothes, passing an endless stream of freshly cooked *mummeliga* (polenta) slabs to the men in the front room, who washed the glutinous maize cakes down with copious drafts of sweet red wine, speaking all the time very sentimentally of the Rumania, *der heim,* that had rejected them so brutally.

As the wine flowed, the men began to sweat: they loosened their waistcoats and freed the top buttons of their trousers. Then they began to sing sad Rumanian peasant songs about unrequited love and my father would take out his mandolin – always the high spot of any family gathering – and start to play. It was an invitation for those ponderous men with moist shining foreheads to dance. They made a ring linking each other's hands across their shoulders and, with surprising grace for their bulk, moved round the room clockwise and withershins, stamping their feet as they sang to the fluctuating rhythm of the *hora* (a Rumanian national dance) long before the Israelis took it as their own.

My mother also was on the short side, but beautifully built. She had a pert, tiptilted nose, sparkling eyes and red cheeks. Till the day she died, after forty years in the slums of the East End, she still had the healthy, fresh-washed look of a buxom dairymaid. She wasn't as well educated as my father. That was because he could afford it, she claimed, as he came from a wealthy family – a Berkovitz was the biggest banker in Rumania. All nonsense, of course. His parents were of common stock. At all events, by the time they married, my father was fairly fluent in English, whereas my mother had just crawled out of the signing-her-name-with-a-cross stage.

But she persevered. Like a lot of other *greeners,* she learnt her English from the silent films. Whenever she could afford it, she took one of us elder children with her to the pictures and we sat through two, and on the Saturday sometimes three, programmes. When a subtitle came on the screen, the first couple of rows spelled it out loudly in unison 'A-N-D T-H-E-N C-A-M-E L-O-V-E', which immediately provoked a sibilant shush of protest from the *literati* at the back.

Painstakingly, mother collected a random list of English words from the dictionary and scribbled them down column after column in a half-penny exercise book. She learned them by heart then garnered another lot. Eventually, she could write a bet to the bookie's satisfaction, and was able to check the results unaided in the Star newspaper. When that day arrived, she had no further use for any scholastic activities.

Within a few years, my father fulfilled his first ambition in London – he had his own tailor's workshop making trousers- but far from being his salvation the workshop proved to be quicksands. Mother and father were in it up to their necks and, as the kids grew up, they were also dragged into the mire. All of us put together couldn't make a decent living. Father borrowed from the city shops to pay the workers. He even used to borrow a few shillings from me to buy cottons and other oddments, but he never paid me back. This led me to hide my pitiful hoard of errand-earned pennies where he couldn't lay hands on it.

He'd had a couple of good seasons to start with, which encouraged him to live in style. He rented three rooms and a workshop, all on the same floor in a tenement house in Bedford Street. Nine of us lived there, *die booba*, mother and father and six children (four boys and two girls). The room facing the street was our parlour and at night it served as a bedroom for the boys. It had an upright piano, which was mandatory in every established Jewish household where there were girls - even if they couldn't play a note. The piano was a caste mark. It showed the owner had triumphantly surmounted the first step towards bourgeois affluence. Every little shopkeeper or struggling master tailor had to have a piano in his house. There might not always be enough to eat in the kitchen but there had to be a piano in the parlour.

My youngest sister, Mary, soon showed that she had a talent for music. She took piano lessons from a visiting teacher, an astringent, old maiden lady, Miss Goldenblatt, from Vorsangers Academy of Music nearby in Philpott Street. Mary delighted the old lady. She had what Miss Goldenblatt termed perfect pitch and remarkable dexterity, and she often stretched the covenanted hour lesson to a couple of hours or more for the same shilling. Even so, Miss Goldenblatt was expensive and not always paid on the nail. My own violin lessons in school cost only three pence per session. But then I was one of a mass production group, whereas Miss Goldenblatt was at least the bespoke trade - Mary got her entire individual attention for the duration.

I gave up the violin pretty quickly. I preferred playing football in the streets with the kids to practising the violin, but Mary loved the piano and adored Miss Goldenblatt and passed every routine musical grade examination like clockwork with no bother at all. The time soon dawned when her tutor confessed she could teach her nothing more. Mary must carry on with advanced tuition, Miss Goldenblatt insisted. She had the makings of a concert virtuoso. It would have taken quite a bit of money and considerable sacrifice on my parents' part to support her while studying in the Paris Conservatoire, Miss Goldenblatt's *alma mater* which, we understood, would have gladly accepted her on the old lady's recommendation. My father, a musician manque himself, was prepared to let her go and my mother finally agreed after laying down a whole series of provisos to protect her daughter's chastity and well-being.

But the whole project fell through. Mary, at fourteen, was well aware of how her parents struggled. For years, she herself had been pressed into service in the workshop after school hours to sew on buttons and trim cotton ends during some busy rush, and resolutely refused to go abroad to continue her studies. She felt that, with everyone else in the family intimately involved, she owed some contribution to the household's maintenance. She therefore got a job as a relief pianist in a newly-built, local super cinema, the Rivoli in Whitechapel Road. The term was exactly what the post implied. When the orchestra finished playing for the long feature film, Mary took over in the pit and supplied the continuous piano obligato to the minor flickerings on the screen, the secondary film, the comedy short, Pathé Gazette, advertising slides and the like. It was a highly-skilled, if lowly paid, occupation, but Mary's musical education had fitted her to undertake it with considerable expertise as, in addition, she was expected to adapt her accompaniment accurately and rhythmically to the action of each frame.

I was in a somewhat similar situation to Mary, also being equipped by nature for better things. In school, I was reckoned to be the brightest boy in my class. My favourite subjects were science and mathematics, but I was also good at history, geography and English. I was a special pet of Taffy Wilson, our science master, a round little Welshman with tousled hair and an innocent expression, like a blue-chinned Rubens cherub.

During physics lessons Taffy would fire apparently unanswerable questions all round the class, while I would squirm in my seat hoping desperately to catch his eye. Finally, he would relent, point to me and rap out "Tell them Barkovitch." He always pronounced my name that way. Proudly I got up and proclaimed: "One cubic centimetre of distilled water at four degrees centigrade equals one gramme." Mr Wilson would nod agreement with a proprietary air, motion me to be seated and say, "Barkovitch, from now on keep quiet for the rest of the lesson. Give the other boys a chance."

As my fourteenth birthday approached Taffy asked me one day to stay behind after class. "Have you made up your mind yet what you're going to do when you leave school?," he asked. "I suppose I'll be going in to my father's workshop." I said.

"Listen to me, Barkovitch," said Mr Wilson. "I've spoken to the headmaster and he agrees with me. We both think you've got too good a brain to waste it in a workshop."

"Thanks for the compliment, Sir," I said. "But there's nothing else I could do with it."

"Indeed there is." Taffy replied. "You can take up science as a career. Wait a moment" – his pudgy hands, always stained brown and green by chemicals, waved my unspoken protestations aside. "I know how you're placed, but I can arrange for you to be employed here in the school for the next couple of years as a pupil teacher. You'll help me in the lab and at the same time be able to continue your studies and you'll be paid seventeen and six a week, so you won't be too much of a burden on your family."

I must have appeared overwhelmed by this generous, and it was indeed quite a magnanimous, offer. With a shy smile Taffy patted me gently on the shoulder and sent me home clutching a letter for my father in which he spelled out his offer in detail.

Mr Wilson's letter got the reception that I expected from my father. He held it in front of my nose. "From that you earn a living?" he asked sarcastically. "Two more, three more years in school working for peanuts and God knows how many more years studying, in college maybe, in university perhaps, before you'll be a *mensch* (a person of integrity and honour) able to make a living and support a family?" he snorted irascibly. "No, Sir! I need you here in the workshop. You must learn a trade. Be a *bulmalocha,* a craftsman. Once you've got a trade in your hands as a *bulmalocha* you'll never starve. You'll make a living wherever you are in the world."

I didn't have the heart to point out that before me stood a highly convincing demolition of his own argument. One good season and my father forgot all those lean years when he was constantly rushing off to the Jewish Board of Guardians for a loan to pay the rent.

But his contemptuous dismissal of the offer was really only rhetoric. If I'd actually wanted to stay on at school, very little persuasion would have been needed. Every orthodox Jew has a deep-seated veneration for learning. In the final analysis, that transcends all financial considerations. But I didn't want to stay on at school. I wanted to be with my contemporaries. They were already earning money in the tailoring workshops. They slouched around the street at nights and weekends, hands in their trousers pockets clinking a few coppers, wearing big caps, with Woodbine cigarettes stuck behind their ears. I too wanted a big cap with a Woodbine stuck behind my ear. I wanted to say goodbye to schooldays.

There was another overriding reason for my father's refusal of Taffy's offer. I didn't know about it at the time, but he was in a hurry. He knew he was going to die soon and he wanted someone to take over the workshop and responsibility for the family. My older brother, Al, had already left home and was making plans to emigrate with his fiancée to America. The two younger boys were still at school, so I was nominated the breadwinner.

When I was seventeen my father died of tuberculosis. He was forty-one. I was now in charge. I kept the workshop going on my own for just over a year and hated every moment I was in it. The only advantage I found in being the boss was that I could instantaneously demote myself to shopboy whenever I felt like it and go out on some footling errand to catch a breath of fresh air or visit the bookie.

It was a constant struggle but we managed to stay solvent – just. It became more and more obvious to me that there was no future in it. My father was a highly skilled worker and he couldn't make a go of it. How then could I, with not one-tenth of his skill or one-hundredth part of his craftsman's dedication, succeed where he had failed? I finally talked mother into selling the entire Berkovitz Bedford Street estate – three rooms and the workshop with all its equipment. None of it belonged to us anyway, apart from the benches, pressing irons and a couple of ancient treadle machines, but my mother got a hundred pounds – a fortune in those days – for the workshop fixtures, fittings and non-existent goodwill.

By then, older brother Al was already in America and married and *die booba* was dead. Mary was busy churning out hearts and flowers in the cinema, my eldest sister was independently employed as a first-class tailoress and the two younger boys, though still at school, were already shaping solidly like future *bulmalochas*.

I convinced mother we would all be better off if the family split up. She would go and live with my sister and the boys in a small flat, and I would get a single room of my own somewhere in the neighbourhood.

My timing was apt, because our local baker, a respectable middle-aged man – Rumanian, naturally – had been to the house a couple of times and was beginning to make overtures of marriage to my elder sister. As for me, I was finalising plans to follow brother Al to America.

Part 2

America

Chapter 6

By 1926 I had accumulated £40. I was free, white, almost twenty-one: it was time to 'go West, young man'. I saved £20 for a ticket to Canada (a year before, I could have got an assisted passage for £10 if I had signed on for the harvest.) The other £20 was to keep me for a month till brother Al made arrangements to smuggle me across the border into the United States as an illegal immigrant.

My ship was the 'Megantic', an intermediate liner of about 17,000 tons. It carried eleven hundred passengers - only a handful of them women – all driven from their own country by economic pressure.

They were artisans and craftsmen from all over the country, all unwanted: miners from Wales and the North, skilled motor mechanics from the Midlands, farmers' boys from the Shires. They were a magnificent bunch of men. Many of them had served in the first World War. The country had no work for them, the government had no use for them, but they were the best crop the land had produced. They were the salt of the earth.

The voyage took ten days: it was a happy ship, full of hope and character. I never heard of anybody having their belongings stolen and there were no attempted rapes or muggings, which would certainly have been a feature of such a crossing fifty years later. The food was stodgy but filling. At any rate, much more generous than anything I was used to.

I shared a cabin with three miners. They were bound for Timmins in Ontario, almost in the Arctic Circle, the northernmost tip of Canada: they had been promised jobs in the lead mines there. The last part of the voyage was pretty cold: I saw my first iceberg jutting out like a miniature mountain peak from the water, a sort of opaque grey-blue in colour, and we had to be led into the St Lawrence River by an ice-breaker.

Montreal was more French than English. I walked round for hours looking for a place where I could flop but I couldn't see any 'apartment vacant' or 'room to let' bills anywhere. At last I asked somebody and he pointed out little 'Maison a Louer' notices tucked away in the windows. I didn't know that in Montreal they spoke as much French as English, maybe more. Anyway, I got a little room in an apartment house and sent a letter off to my brother. A day or two later he wrote telling me to hang on till he had made all necessary arrangements. He enclosed a fifty dollar bill to keep me going.

I had nothing else to do but mooch around the city all day long. I went to the movies once or twice nearly every day and shared the rest of the day between cheap cafeterias and park benches. When the parks were closed there was nothing for it but more movies or bed, so I usually went to bed early, but that turned out to be as broad as it was long, because I woke up soon after dawn and couldn't sleep any more.

Within a week or so my dollars ran out. I wrote my brother and he sent me another twenty dollars by registered post.

At that time the one topic in Montreal was the General Strike in England. I used to hang around newspaper offices and watch the latest bulletins in the windows. There was a large white sheet stretched taut across the full width of the window while the machines tapped out the messages in big block letters as they flashed through.

I hadn't expected to stay in Montreal more than a week or so, but there wasn't any word from my brother, so to make my money last I moved to the top floor of the apartment house where I shared a sort of dormitory with four others. Then, three or four weeks later, my brother wrote to me to go to Niagara Falls, the Canadian side. A couple of his friends would meet me there and show me the ropes. They would be in a green Buick tourer and he gave me the number to watch out for. I checked out and took my bag, with nothing in it but a change of underclothes, and got the train to Niagara.

I waited there for two solid days, but there was no sign of a green Buick. Somehow, I'd missed them. I became disheartened; after all, I was only a youngster. I thought they had forgotten me, or maybe hadn't troubled. All through the day I hung round by the Falls near the International Bridge. I had a crazy notion to swim across to the other side. I bought a tough plaited rope. The idea was to fix it to a tree and pay it out as I progressed, trusting to the current to wash me on to the opposite bank. Reconnoitering one of the deep gorges looking for a suitable spot to start from, I saw a monument. It was to a Cincinnati youth who dived in to save a young couple but had got drowned along with the other two. That put me off. I wasn't hankering for any monument of that sort.

I decided the best and sanest thing to do would be to get back to Montreal, where the landlord welcomed me back without any surprise. I sat down straight away and wrote another letter to my brother to find out what was happening. The reply told me his friends had arrived but, owing to some delay had got to Niagara a day late and had just missed me. It was my own fault. I shouldn't have been so impatient. He felt like washing his hands of me and telling me to get the hell back to England. But a brother is a brother after all; he sent me fifteen bucks as well, and told me to wait and not be in such a damned hurry, and not to make any mistakes next time because it was my last chance.

Two weeks later, I got the message to meet the Buick again. This time it came off as arranged. One of my brother's friends gave me his bridge pass, and they both spent a couple of hours putting me through a sort of rehearsal, in case the bridge officials asked any questions.

The plan was to say I was from Buffalo. I didn't live there, I worked there. I came from Scranton, Pennsylvania. Scranton because that was a long way off, and the guards weren't likely to know anything about that place. If they asked me what were the last letters of the alphabet – a favourite trick – I was to say X,Y, Zee not X,Y, Zed. I learned it all pat. They changed my Canadian money into USA currency and wished me luck.

I stepped onto the bridge and, walking towards the United States, was stopped at the turnstile. The officials could have smelt I was an emigrant. I was a raw boy, obviously English from my clothes, and very East London-ish at that. In fact, I took my cap off when I approached them and rested it lightly on the ledge by the turnstiles when I stopped, with the lining upwards and there, right in the middle was a white label with the name Zissman, and the shop's Whitechapel address in bold black lettering. I quickly covered the label with my fist and pulled myself together. I had enough sense not to try and put on a Yankee accent because I knew that I'd only forget myself in the excitement and start jawing in my usual Cockney. "Bridge pass?" I fumbled in my pockets and brought out, as if by mistake, the Buffalo trolleycar return ticket the boys had given me. I took care that the officials had a good look at it before I put it back and got out the pass. I hoped that would convince them that I was from Buffalo. Besides, the car I had just got out of had an American registration number and in any case, they could see the driver was a Yank with their eyes shut.

By this time, about half a dozen other officials had gathered round. There were no automobiles waiting and I was the only pedestrian. They had nothing else to do, and wanted some sport. I couldn't have chosen a worse time to cross.

"Where you from?" one fired at me.

"Buffalo," I replied

"Live there?"

"No. Work there."

"What's your home town?"

"Scranton, Pennsylvania."

"From the diamond mines, huh?"

I grinned and dismissed it with "Yeah. Black diamonds." I still remembered enough geography to know that Pennsylvania was famous for its coalmines and thanked my lucky stars I had taken my lessons seriously in school and been an attentive kid.

"You know Latzo?" one of the officials asked, winking at the others.

"Sure I know Latzo," I answered, "I used to spar with him at the club." It was a real bit of luck. When the boys told me to mention Scranton, they didn't dream the bridge officials would link up the name with Pete Latzo, the boxer. He was a Scranton miner who had recently fought for the welter-weight championship and being a bit of a fight fan myself and having nothing much else to do, I had read about a dozen different accounts of the fight while I was awaiting my tryst with the Buick. When they mentioned Latzo I felt as if they'd named an old pal and it came out so naturally that they didn't know what to say. In my excitement I elbowed my way past them and they didn't even attempt to stop me.

I strolled down the bridge not daring to look back and expecting any minute a tap on the shoulder and one of those huskies saying: "This way sonny!" But nothing happened. I got to the end of the bridge, safely in the United States. Taking the first turning to the right like the boys had advised, I almost fell into a drugstore, where I bought a pick-me-up, and sat down for a while. After that, I felt better. Later, when I was on the New York train, I learned they had caught eleven emigrants that day. Why I didn't make it twelve I still can't understand.

Brother Al met me at Grand Central station in New York and whisked me off in a cab to his flat in the Bronx. His wife Polly, a very pleasant little lady, made me feel at home immediately. A meal, a bath and a rest, then Al took me to the neighbourhood cinema, where I had my first taste of the prodigal richness of American entertainment. A feature film, a sports short, a comedy, the newsreel and, live on stage eight, first-rate vaudeville acts – a close on four-hour show viewed from a comfortable seat with cigar and popcorn all for less than a dollar.

Next morning Al kitted me out with one of his suits, a light-weight navy blue alpaca and crowned it with a straw boater with a dashing striped silk band. It was Thursday: I would spend the rest of the week finding my bearings and acclimatising myself to the terrain. From next Monday I'd start thinking about a job.

I was drunk with New York. Transport was cheap, 8 miles on the subway for a nickel – tuppence ha'penny – but I walked everywhere, indulging in my favourite pastime. When I was a kid in London I used to take long rambles with my friend Hymie Olinsky round the city and many times passed a historical church, St Ethelburga, in Bishopsgate. The English navigator Richard Hudson had gone there to have his mission to America blessed and it was here in New York four hundred years later that – albeit without benefit of clergy – I walked along the built-up banks of the river named after him.

I think one reason I liked New York so much was its closeness to water. Wherever you went you weren't far from the river or the sea. Manhattan, after all, is an island. It diverts the Hudson river at its mouth. It runs north to south, on its west is North River and to the south, East River. It comprises five boroughs, Manhattan, The Bronx, Staten Island and Kings and Queens, both in Brooklyn.

The wide, straight avenues ride the city from north to south and the streets cross the avenues from east to west. Broadway is generally regarded as bisecting the city, but I found it was not truly central as it moved diagonally. It made 42nd Street and Times Square the genuine centre of the city for me and, in my rubber-necking euphoria, the centre of the entire civilised world. It was the tenderloin district around Murray Hill and from 42nd to 50th Street, roughly a square mile, and it seemed as familiar to me as Whitechapel. It was Gotham City-Baghdad on the subway. Here were the hustlers, the conmen, the gamblers, the brisk movers and fast talkers I recognised from the movies and from O. Henry short stories.

The generally buoyant atmosphere of New York in 1926 I found to be in sharp contrast to the depressed mood of the London I had left a few weeks before. There were no dole queues outside Labour exchanges. No battalions of beggars. Only the odd hard core, utterly down-and-out, Bowery types. Food was good and, along with services, surprisingly cheap. The people never drifted aimlessly about the streets as in London, but were always bustling along purposefully, and were neat and well-dressed.

The ebullient public figures I watched mounting and ceaselessly descending the stairs of City Hall were particularly well-groomed. As a tailor I could appreciate the skilled cut of their clothes. The neatly turned hand-stitched lapels, the knife-edged creases in their trousers, I compared most favourably with the crumpled black jackets and waistcoats and baggy striped trousers of the seedy representatives of the British electorate I had left behind in London. Only a couple of years later, however, on my second visit, I was to discover that these natty New York dressers were an even bigger bunch of deadbeats than our own shabby creeps and just as criminally negligent in their treatment of the unemployed. Worse, they were hollow men. These New World leaders were bagmen for the gangsters, actually working closely in association with The Syndicate, for whom they leaned on judges and police and in return got money, votes and political support.

In those first days, and to a lesser degree during the next three months, I explored this relentlessly occupied metropolis from end to end. It fascinated me and, despite its current dirt and dangers, the city fascinates me still. In 1926 I was part of New York while it was growing up and still as it had been during the past thirty years. There was yet no Chrysler Building, the East River bridges were practically new and skyscrapers reached no higher than 20 or 30 storeys.

I loved the polyglot, Lower East Side with Italian, Polish, Yiddish and German heard on the streets as much as English. With every type of restaurant offering cheese blintzes, stuffed neck, and gefilte fish like your mother used to make. With bakery windows heaped with stacks of bagels, pretzels and 30 different kinds of bread. And everywhere the automats, supreme example of American inventive genius, selling the choicest, ready-cooked food in New York and the best blueberry pies anywhere.

There were, of course, the usual let-downs. Broadway I found to be anything but a Great White Way. It was distinctly tawdry compared with London's smart (even during the Depression) West End. The Bowery, on the other hand, was nothing like the shabby skid row I'd expected. Instead of a mean little street, I discovered a wide, very much alive thoroughfare with four sets of trolley car tracks and a railway, the Elevated, or L, clattering overhead. The buildings looked as if they hadn't had a lick of paint in years, but the retail shops and warehouses all seemed to be doing pretty well.

The Salvation Army had taken over the ground floor of one decaying Bowery warehouse, and converted it into a citadel. A huge flag embossed with the Army's crest in black, red and gold hung outside and in the window was a big sign:

SOAP

SOUP

SALVATION

Underneath the sign was a legend in smaller letters:

Have you written to your mother?

Let us help.

Come inside for tea, envelope and stamp.

I also found on the Bowery a nationally famous institution, "The Cooper Union," doing the same sort of work our own Quintin Hogg had started with his Regent Street Polytechnic. It offered working people a technical and scientific education after normal working hours and obligingly tailored, where possible, day class times to suit their needs. This was for me, I decided. It struck a responsive chord built in my hungry-for-learning background. Once I had settled in I would look the Cooper Union over seriously and do whatever was necessary to join.

Four days of unclouded highs ended on Sunday. On Monday the lows took over and continued through the week thereafter, with unrelenting frequency. I wasn't only the forgotten man, but the unwanted man as well. I got up in the morning, devoured the six Situations Vacant columns in the 'World' and, picking up other discarded journals in the subway *en route*, rushed off to the ringed addresses. At the end of the week, however, with not a single solid offer for my services, I could not help but appear despondent. I didn't have to spell it out for brother Al.

"Snap out of it Sam," he said. "Everyone gets a job in New York eventually."

"Eventually?" I echoed glumly.

"Sure," said Al. "And you'll stay here with us for as long as it takes."

"You know you're very welcome," sister-in-law Polly assured me. She flashed her conspiratorial smile. "Fancy a cup of tea, Sam?"

"Not tonight Josephine," said Al. "No tea." He took out a bottle of Scotch whisky from a cupboard – no bathtub hooch - but the genuine article straight off the boat via a sailor friend. It was kept for special occasions and tonight, Al decided, was a special occasion. He poured a shot for me and one for himself. *"Lechaim,"* (to Life) he said and, clinking glasses, we tossed he liquor down swallow for swallow.

"Now come on." Al put on his jacket. "We're going to the movies. Just the two of us. Polly's been. She says it's a great show." As I reached for my hat he slapped me on the back. "Smile, damn you, smile! You're a Berkovitz. Our old man walked halfway across Europe just to get to London. T'aint the end of the world, Sam!"

That night I took stock of the situation. Al was only just over a year older than me, and Polly was even closer my age. Yet they had taken it on themselves to look after me *in loco parentis* as they say in the classics. But I was an independent sort of cuss. I had to do everything for myself. I figured the world might owe me a living, but not my relatives and friends.

Al had the advantage over me in the battle for survival in New York. He was a real craftsman. He had a wife and a job. I had no saleable skills to peddle, not even trousers making. There were perhaps half a dozen trouser lofts (the American term for workshop) in the whole of New York – if you knew where to find them – as against the scores of little workshops in London.

American trousers were mainly produced in large factories, the highly specialised one-section-of-the-job-per-operator system, presenting no difficulty to me with my all-round home training. The trouble was getting into the factory. I had no union card and with no money to spread around in graft to get one, and with no personal contacts on that side of the industry to obtain a card legitimately, that avenue was securely closed.

Al worked for a small shop in the bespoke end of the trade that wasn't yet completely unionised and where, in any case, his special skill as a cutter was as rare as rubies – though they paid him in potatoes. With all his expertise, he never earned more than forty dollars a week while he worked in New York.

It boiled down to finding semi or unskilled work, shipping clerk, short-order cook or counterhand but, whenever I got to the first job advert in the 'World' magazine, there was always half a dozen there before me and when I arrived at the next on the list, a queue was already forming.

Getting up earlier wouldn't do the trick either. I was already awake practically at the crack of dawn as soon as the 'World' tumbled through the letter box. But I lived in the Bronx and most of the jobs were the other end of town. No doubt there were other applicants from the Bronx but they had already become Americanised, infected with the New World's rush, while I still maintained my leisurely European tempo.

These other job seekers had inherited the traditions of the Jewish immigrants of the eighties and nineties, with 'Work Hard!' as their gospel. Al showed me a little guide book in Yiddish issued to such immigrants on arrival. He called it the *Loifer's Charter*. *'Loif'* means run and its message begins: '*Loif!* Take not a moment's rest. Work! Keep your own and your children's good always in mind!'

I did, however, get quite a number of interviews – mainly with 'mockies', as the natives disparagingly called foreigners. Strangely, it didn't occur to me that I was a mockie myself, and they were as suspicious of me as I was of them. There was something not quite *kosher* about me. I spoke a Whitechapel English that probably sounded like Harvard in their ears and I could read and write. With such high-class qualifications, looking for a job keeping a drugstore counter tidy indicated there must be something wrong. Probably I was a crook. Maybe on the run from the police, which in a sense I was, as any confrontation with the law would have got me expelled from the country as an illegal immigrant.

I decided that this was about as low down the employment scale as I was prepared to go. There were plenty of restaurant, busboy and dishwasher jobs around, but they only paid about thirty cents an hour, less than the equivalent of one shilling and tenpence ha'penny per hour I could earn in London.

Nor did the Horatio Alger rags to riches stories inspire me. There were no doubt genuine examples around of people starting in similar humble circumstances, saving their cents, working extra long and hard, and shrewdly investing their sweat until they could bankroll the dollars into millions. That took too long. I didn't have time. That's the paradox of youth. With all the time in the world, there's never enough time. No Sir, I said to myself, none of this long-term drudgery for me. I haven't come to America to slave for a pittance less than in London. I have 'come to thrive it wealthily in Padua'.

I had to admit defeat in my earliest skirmishes. I had lost the first battle – though not yet perhaps the war. True, I hadn't expected to be greeted by an army of bosses marching down Broadway with banners, crying 'We want Sam,' but I had been pretty certain that some sort of opening would have presented itself by now. Already I knew that this sortie to the States was doomed. I'd give it another few weeks and then go home and prepare myself properly for a second assault on New York. I had learned the hard way what my reading of military history in Whitechapel library should have prepared me for in theory. I shouldn't have launched myself on foreign shores without studying beforehand the terrain, the manners and mores of the inhabitants. I didn't know the language and I lacked the drive and pushiness of the natives. I could read and write good English, but I had no real education, no university degrees. My endeavours in the employment field were therefore strictly limited. I couldn't undertake any responsible job because, as an illegal immigrant, I couldn't provide character references or find anyone to be surety for a bond if one were required.

Facing the truth, however unpalatable, was a relief. It was like being told of a terminal illness after years of niggling uncertainty. I knew what had to be done. I had to get an education. It was there: The Cooper Union, and I had to become a citizen and enter the United States by the front door on the English immigrant quota.

Chapter 7

In my third week of unemployment, I became a *schlepper*. Barney instructed me in my duties. He had smooth, black, Brilliantined hair and was altogether sleek, round and shining, like a plum pudding. He owned a small tailor's shop near Washington Avenue and, being in the same line of business, was a sort of buddy of brother Al's.

"Dust de shelves," he told me. "See de garments ain't squeezed too close on de racks? When you spot a customer in de street, *schlep* him in and leave de rest to me." I'd only taken the job as a token to show I was willing. And Barney had only given it to me to oblige brother Al. But it was a disaster from the start. When I saw someone looking in the window I approached with a diffident "Can I help you, Sir?" The genuine *schlepper's modus operandi* would have been to take him gently but firmly by the sleeve and propel him into the store to the accompaniment of a non-stop *spiel*.

Tackling a couple of likely prospects with the hearty approach "Can I be of any assistance gentlemen?" they reared like frightened fauns, turned tail without a word and fled. Barney noticed. "Why didn't you *schlep* them in?" he demanded. "They said they weren't interested." "Den why was dey looking in de window?" he asked.

It was no use beating about the bush. I could see we weren't meant for each other. The same stupid pride that held me from asking for, or accepting, assistance from relatives kept me from badgering these other guys who, I felt, had a right to make up their minds on their own, even if they did stop to look at a suit in the window. Barney sorrowfully shook his shining head, took out a bill fold and peeled off a couple of small ones. "Here's two dollars. Dat's for expenses." He took my hand in a friendly grasp. "Tell Al I'm sorry." "Me too," I said.

With an extra couple of bucks in my pocket and half a working day left to kill, I resumed my leisurely tour of New York. As usual, I soon found myself back on the East Side, wandering down the Bowery. On an impulse, I stopped by the Apex Employment Agency. Only a grubby shack despite its posh title, it was one of a number in the area. I had often seen bunches of shabby men gathered round a vacancies board on the sidewalk outside. Today there was nobody there, so I turned the handle of the door and went in. It was a big gloomy room lined with wooden benches like a hospital outpatients. There were several large blackboards attached to the walls smudged with rubbed out chalk marks under permanent white ruled work headings.

A middle-aged man in a once white sweat shirt was sitting at a desk immersed in a racing sheet. An unlit, half-smoked stogie dripping little spirals of wet tobacco was gripped between his teeth. Overhead, a large electric fan the size of an aeroplane propeller was suspended from the ceiling, squeezing out small groans after each revolution, like the straining timbers of a ship. It was similar to a scene from a hundred East of Suez 'B' movies.

The man looked up as I walked in. "Yeah?" "Good afternoon," I mumbled.

"Yeah?"

He had short cropped, curly brown hair flecked with grey and a massive head sprouting straight out of enormous shoulders. His face, his neck, his arms and the top of his chest glistened with sweat.

He had a small pug nose and little watery blue eyes that fixed me with a cold, unflinching stare.

"I've come about a job," I said.

He chewed the stogie to the corner of his mouth, picked up a stub of pencil which looked sadly lost in his pudgy fist and held it poised ready to write.

"Name?"

"Berkovitz."

"Pollak?"

"No. I'm from London."

"Limey?" He looked puzzled. "Wid a name like Berkovitz?"

"I'm Jewish," I explained.

"Ah!" He tossed the pencil stub back on the desk. His shrewd eyes ranged over me from top to toe appraising the puny physique beneath the sharp alpaca suit.

"You speak good," he said noncommittally. "You read and write?" "Sure," I nodded.

"Den what de hell you doin' here?"

"This is an employment agency isn't it?" I retorted. "Says Apex Employment outside." "So?"

"So? I've come about employment. I want a job. Like all the other bums who come here." Immediately he bridled. He flung a beefy arm across the desk and inclined his thick torso to follow it. "Dem bums ain't bums!" he growled belligerently. "Dem bums is migrant workers."

Slightly mollified by my cowed expression, he bothered to explain. Apex catered for unskilled labourers who travelled from job to job mainly on railway construction. They would be hired on the Bowery, ferried out to camps on site and live there until the job was completed.

"You ever done dat type work? Twelve hours a day wid pick and shovel?," he demanded.

"No," I said. But I could try."

"Don't be a dope, son," he said. "You ain't got de muscle for dat type job. It'd kill you in two weeks."

"What's the pay?," I insisted.

"Usual. 30 cents an hour. "But" – he was thoughtful – "If you need a job dat bad I could maybe sign you up in camp as flunkey."

"What do you mean flunkey?"

"You should know," he said. "You're from England." All de top brass dere got flunkeys – dey fetch and carry, cook hash, wash dishes."

"What's the pay?" I asked

"Same," he said. "Longer hours but works out de same. 30 cents widout your keep."

I didn't answer immediately. To the man it must have seemed I was trying to make up my mind.

He did it for me. He waved his hand dismissively and picked up the scratch sheet.

"Beat it, bud," he said, not unkindly. "Nuffing here for you. You read and write. Plenty joints need clerks – warehouses, banks. Scram son. I'm busy."

The stogie swung back to its previous position clamped centrally in the greasy lipless mouth. The interview was over. I left.

Chapter 8

My first real job in New York came quite by accident. I had stopped on the sidewalk to buy some smokes and a drink of orange juice at a Nedick's booth and got into casual conversation with another customer. It turned out he was a Londoner too, Danny Greene, the son of an Irish dock labourer from Shadwell. A chunky, open-faced, middle-aged man, he had served his time as a boy soldier and came to America in 1920. Now, he told me proudly, he was the superintendent of an apartment block on 27th Street; what was more, if I wanted a job there I could have it.

"As what?" I asked.

"Janitor. The pay's lousy" he admitted, but the work's easy and there's opportunities."

"What opportunities?"

"To make something of yourself, like Milton," he said.

"Milton wasn't the poet, he was Milton Goldstein, another Jewish lad from Boston, who was studying medicine at Columbia University. That was during the day. At night, Milton was also a Janitor at the 27th Street apartments.

"But first, forget about tailoring," Danny said. "*Schneidereis,* that's strictly for the old 'mockies'. This is a technological age. The era of wireless, electro-mechanics, planned circuitry. You interested in radio?" he threw in. "Know anything about mathematics?"

I nodded. "In school that was one of my favourite subjects."

"So what are you waiting for?" Danny asked. "The Cooper Union's right on your doorstep. In your own spare time you can learn a new trade, a modern trade. Master it and you'll never starve wherever you are in the world." He looked at me suspiciously. "What are you grinning at? What I'm saying is not funny."

"Sure ain't." I said. "Quite the contrary. My father used the same expression." "Your father was a very wise man," Danny agreed.

That was Tuesday. Early next morning I reported for duty. Danny was right: the duties were not onerous, simply boring. I had breakfast about 7.15, emptied the ash cans and took over the lift and switchboard at 8 a.m. I worked right through to 6 p.m., having lunch on the hop. Then Milton came back from college and took over till midnight. We both slept in the same room, but had nothing much else in common.

Milton had vaguely radical sympathies, but knew as much about the England I had just left as I did about the Great Wall of China. He wasn't the least bit interested in learning any more either. Milton's only concern was passing his exams and becoming Dr Goldstein.

Danny was possessed of a daemonic energy. He was up, washed, shaved and dressed before anyone else in the block was stirring and went to bed long after the last bumps and bangs and furtive shuffles of night were stilled. In between, he never seemed to rest and even when his body was inactive his tongue was working nineteen to the dozen. Danny was a dyed-in-the-wool Republican. Though born in Stepney, he hated London. He detested the British. They'd treated him all his life like a second-class citizen, he claimed. The whole of Britain was *kaput*. It deserved all it got – and more. America was different. It was the land of opportunity. "I came here with nothing," he kept boasting. "Look at me now – and the way I'm going I'll even end up a millionaire."

Danny's first job in America had also been as a liftman servicing a building that housed a number of lofts. The liftmen were *ganzer muchers* – the wheeler-dealers of the neighbourhood. Danny used to run the 'totsies' special'. On pay days, he cruised prostitutes between the floors and stopped at loft entrances to enquire "Anyone want a piece of ass for a buck?" Takers would be hoisted to the top floor where Danny held the lift incommunicado while they did their business on the floor.

On Friday night Milton went home, his weekend off, and I was faced with 36 hours continuous duty, on call all the time. There would be no four-hour jaunts about the city, no free time to sit and think or read. There would only be Danny, endlessly hating the British and reapportioning the six counties. It was more than I could endure. I told Danny I was packing up on Sunday night. He seemed genuinely sorry but didn't appear surprised.

"You're a funny fellow, Sam," he said. "You've got no *sitzfleisch*". Danny loved to flaunt the odd Yiddish word he'd picked up from his tenants. "You won't stay put awhile, yet there's no 'get up and go' either. 'Get up and go,' that's what you need, but looks like you don't care at all if you make the grade or not." He shook my hand. *"Gay gezunt.* Go in good health. Here's your *gelt* and a five-spot extra. But take my advice. Join the Cooper Union. And if you change your mind about working and spare time study, come and see me. I'll be here."

I still had a couple of aces up my sleeve. One was the business address of a young man I had met in Canada while I was scouting round the Falls. We were sharing a table in a café and I pointed out of the window to a great forest of chimneys belching black smoke on the opposite bank.

"Look at them," I commented smugly, 'They're like the Falls, also brute power, but controlled by man, not let loose by nature."

He nodded agreement. "You know what they are? Where they are?" I had to confess ignorance on both counts.

"That's Buffalo, America," he said. 'The chimneys are Bethlehem, a division of United Steel. I've just come from there. On business."

He was a crew-cut, college type WASP from New York. About 29 or 30. Well-built, well dressed and well spoken. He seemed intrigued by my accent, my vocabulary and the reason for my trip to Niagara. He'd even offered to run me across the border in his car. To him the whole thing was a bit of a joke. The guards would just wave through an obviously well-heeled American in a sleek Buick and not look twice at the nondescript young man sitting at his side. Even if they didn't, he was cheerfully prepared to take a chance. My idiotic scruples, however, stopped me from saying yes. I told him I was supposed to meet a friend of my brother's who would be disturbed if I didn't show up.

He gave me his card before we parted. He was in gelatine foods and had an office on the West 60s. I passed the building a dozen times during the first jobless month I was in New York and each occasion increased my reluctance to get someone so well-intentioned into any sort of trouble on my account, till I finally gave up the idea altogether.

My last card was my pal Solly Schwartz's aunt. I'd met her briefly at Solly's house in Stepney a couple of years previously. We'd exchanged a few words and I promised to look her up whenever I got to America.

I rang the bell of her house, a solid, three storey, brownstone building in Yorkville by the East 60s. Nothing happened. I waited and rang the bell again. I thought maybe I'd got the wrong address and checked in my notebook. It was her place all right. Then I said to myself I should have got her phone number from information and called first, to save her any inconvenience and me a journey. Undecided whether to leave right away or stay a little longer, I noticed a small grille sliding open in the heavy door. As I'd only gone there against my own inclination and better judgement, I had an impulse to forget the whole thing and go home even then. But I thought, what the hell – she can't eat me – and I'm here now anyway. I approached closer to the grille. A large, red-rimmed eye looked out and an easily remembered voice, even though I had only heard it once before, growled "Oo you?"

I said, "Sam Berkovitz."

"Sam oo?"

"Berkovitz – Sam Berkovitz."

"Vat you vant?"

"You said I should call on you."

The voice was mystified. "I said? Me?"

"In London," I told her. "When I come to America you said I should call on you for a job."

"A jubb? – Me?" The deep voice still wasn't convinced.

"You said your husband Morton would find me a job."

"Ah, Morton," she said softly. Then there was a sudden return of suspicion and a sharpening of tone. "Ow you gut mine address?"

"Your nephew. My pal Solly. Solly Schwartz gave it to me," I replied.

"Ah," she said "Vait, I vill let you in."

There was a muffled clanking as a heavy chain unhooked and I passed into a large, gloomy hall. Solly's aunt closed the door behind me carefully, shut the grille and hooked back the chain. She turned and gave me a thorough inspection. Apparently satisfied, she motioned me to follow her into the lounge.

"Zitz," she said, waving towards a chair. "Siddown. You vill eat somet'ing?"

"No thanks." I said. "I'm not hungry."

She seated herself opposite me, breathless from the exertion, with a round, glass-topped occasional table with curved gilt legs between us.

"A schnaps, yes? Visky? You like Bourbon?" she wheezed, in that unmistakable throaty contralto.

I shook my head. "No. Really."

"A coffee, mit cookies, yes? Dese kichlech I make mineself. De best fahm eggs, de best butter. De best ingredients vat money can buy. Mine cookies dey melt in de maut. Dis I guarantee." she said.

I hesitated: "Well…If it's not too much trouble…."

"Trobble?" she said. "Vat trobble? – I gut servants." She gripped the arms of her chair and levered her great weight to her feet. Standing, she put a podgy finger to her lips – "Shuh!" she whispered conspiratorily. "Shtoom!"

Both of us froze for a moment in silence, then she lowered herself back in her seat. "Mine maid" she explained, "Die schvartze. Everybody vat comes she's gut to know oo day are." She tilted her head away from me and bawled towards the door: "Lorraine! Lorraine!" An elderly black lady wearing a starched white apron above a dark dress with white lace collar and cuffs appeared. She gave me a friendly gap-toothed grin.

"Yes-um," she said.

"Cup coffe. Mit cookies. Mine vat I make. Not de shop vuns." Lorraine nodded, grinned again, and disappeared.

"Dat Lorraine," muttered Solly's aunt. "A fire on 'er! I treat 'er like mine own dotter. Give 'er clothes, parcels, food for de children. And yet she steals everyt'ing she can lay on de 'ands. She's a gunef, a thief. She 'ates me like poison. To tell you de true, I am frightened from 'er. She vill do me a mischief. Vun day I vill vake up and find myself dead mit a knife in de back – you'll see!"

I tried to bring her round to the purpose of my visit – "Would it be possible for me to see your husband?" I asked

Again, the suspicious tone cropped up – "Vy?"

"I told you. About a job."

"Oh yaas – a jubb. Ow long you bin in America?"

"Seven weeks – two months nearly. I thought your husband might know of something."

"Vat something?"

"Work. Anything." I said. "I'm sure if I spoke to him......is it possible?"

"No," she said. "Mine Morton is not in de house."

"Shall I wait? – Can I come back?"

"You ken vait and you ken come back. Do vat you like. But you von't see him." She turned on me her large, wet, calculating gaze. "Mine Morton is not in New York" she announced finally. "He is in Georgia."

"On business, I suppose?"

She flared up bitterly. "Some business! Mit American gunef? – dey're all gunovim – gangsters – a fire on dem all!"

"Any idea when he'll be back?"

She raised her drooping shoulders, quietening down. "Oo knows 'ow long such a business takes?"

After coffee and cakes, I left. Not exactly empty-handed. Solly's aunt gave me her card and told me to present it to her nephew,

Walter Simpson. He might be able to help. Nephew Walter, she told me, ran a large brokerage concern in the Wall Street area.

She wasn't kidding either. This Simpson occupied two whole floors of the Watson building in Broad Street off the Battery. I was there within the hour. "I want to see Mr Walter Simpson," I told the attractive young clerk at the enquiries desk.

"For what purpose, may I ask?" Her voice like her appearance, was crisp, cool and efficient. "For the purpose of employment." I said.

"Do you have an appointment?" I shook my head. "No."

She gave me a form and indicated a vacant chair by a table in the outer office. "Fill in this questionnaire. It will be passed on to Personnel."

I got as far as writing down my name and address and that was about it. The rest asked about previous employers, university degrees, etc. etc. I took the form back to the enquiries clerk. She looked at it and looked at me.

"You haven't filled it in." she said, snootily. "What's the problem?"

"No problem," I told her. "Just pass it on to Mr Simpson with this card."

She peered at the blank questionnaire dubiously and at the card which obviously meant nothing to her. "Well – I don't know....', she hesitated. "Excuse me a moment." She swept up card and questionnaire, left the desk and disappeared into the inner office. A few moments later she was back, smiling, her whole attitude changed. "Mr Simpson will see you now, Sir. Come this way please."

Walter Simpson behind his gleaming mahogany desk, its green polished leather top the size of a ping-pong table, looked like a darker, ten years older version of my friend from Niagara, clean cut, well laundered, sprucely barbered. He held the card between the finger and thumb of one hand.

The questionnaire he held in the other.

"So, you know my aunt?" he said.

"I met her, once, in London." I replied.

He lifted his eyebrows. "You're from London?"

I nodded. "Her nephew Solly Schwartz is a great friend of mine. We went to school together." "I know the Schwartzes." he said. "Perhaps know of" would be better. But what's the connection with my aunt?"

"No connection, except that she told me to look her up when I got to America and she'd help me find a job."

He was thoughtful. "I see. Well, I'll help if I can. What can you do? Know anything about the brokerage business?"

"Not a darn thing"' I admitted cheerfully. "I'm a trousers maker."

He grinned. "Well as you see, we don't make trousers here. How do you think we could be of use? Know anything about book keeping? Double entry? Done any clerical work?"

"No.... never."

"Now be honest. You want a job here. Doing what? Apart from licking stamps and running errands – and you're too old, or too young for that – what can you do?"

I shrugged my shoulders. "Nothing."

He rose to his feet and held out his hand. "Sorry, Sam. You see how it is. Nice to have met you." We shook hands and I walked to the door. "By the way," he called after me, "When you write to the Schwartzes give them my best regards."

When I told brother Al about Solly's aunt he laughed like a drain. He knew all about 'mine Morton'. He'd had a whole page to himself with pictures in the yellow 'Graphic' some six months before. Morton was in Georgia, all right, in the Penitentiary in Atlanta. Apparently, he had been shopped to the Feds by some disgruntled bootleg business associates and was sent down for tax evasion. According to Al, Morton had been lucky not to find a more permanent resting place, cocooned in cement at the bottom of the East River.

Within a month, brother Al's sailor buddy had arranged for me to work my passage back to England on his ship as a seamen's mess steward. The trip took ten days. We called at Plymouth and Le Havre and discharged our final cargo in London, at the George V docks a few minutes' train-ride from my mother's house.

Chapter 9

Two years later, in 1928, I was back in the Big Apple. Not on my own this time. My best friend Hymie Olinsky couldn't leave London because of family ties, but another school chum, Harry Singer, accompanied me.

It was a dreary, rough passage on the 53,000 tons 'Berengaria,' formerly the German liner 'Vaterland.' Six days of violent seas and squally weather. On the afternoon of November 4, 1928, we docked at pier 54 on Manhattan's West Side.

Gripping our cardboard suitcases, we walked to Union Square and took the subway to Prospect Parkway where a cousin of Harry's lived – by this time a disillusioned brother Al had already returned to England with Polly. After we had freshened up, Harry's cousin gave us a nice cooked meal and her husband took us to our lodgings at the home of friends, a sweet, elderly Jewish couple called Lewis in Douglas Street. The room was nothing spectacular. Neat and clean with a washbasin, towels and two single beds. The rent was $17 a month for the two of us. I lodged there quite happily for about eighteen months with Harry and when he eventually left to go back to England on his own, the kindly Mrs Lewis, without any prompting from me, reduced the room rent from $17 to $12.

My friend Harry Singer was an all-round tailor, an impeccable *Bulmalocha*. He found a job within a few days as a bushelman in a busy retail shop altering off-the-peg clothes to fit the individual customer. He shortened or lengthened sleeves and trousers, let out or took in seams, raised or lowered collars. He was busy as a beaver all the time, and loved it.

A short, swarthy, square-shouldered young man, Harry was even busy during any leisure hours at home: his hands always had to be occupied. His half of the room was as shining as a bandbox, and he'd have titillated up my half too if I'd allowed it. He was just as finicky about his personal appearance. At night he not only put his pants in a press, but ironed out creases in his underwear.

Inside a week I too found work, in a sports store off Broadway. They made and marketed all types of athletic accessories. My job was to cut jockstraps and running shorts. My pay, roughly the same as Harry's, was $22, so with close on $180 a month coming in between us, we were in clover.

Before the first month was up I was fired. My boss came up to the cutting table and said, "Sam, you've got to go. Take your time." – which didn't mean take your time at all, but exactly the opposite. Go now!

For all his harshness, my boss was a decent sort. He even bothered to explain: "I don't understand it," he said. "This is usually our busiest time. Today, there's not a single order on the books and I've got enough stock made up to furnish the Olympics!"

Actually, I wasn't too bothered by my speedy departure. It didn't affect my master plan. There was plenty of unskilled work around. If I couldn't find anything in my own trade right away, I would reconnoitre the entire employment field. That might take six months to a year. Meantime, there was the Cooper Union. Properly pursued, that plan was going to transform me into a card holding member of the American technocracy, a fully-fledged electrical engineer.

My next job was on Wall Street, where I mingled with the richest men in America. My pay was 30 cents an hour. I was a messenger for Western Union's Wall Street office. It was casual work. You could work for as little or as long as you liked. I usually put in a ten-hour day, eating on the trot. So long as I was visible and physically available at the office, these brief coffee breaks didn't rate any salary deduction. I made $3 a day five days a week - $15 (then about £3.15 shillings) enough to keep me reasonably comfortable.

In the '20s, 30 cents an hour seemed to be the standard American labourer's wage. Even some semi-skilled car workers in Detroit factories – not yet unionized – got 30 cents an hour. Down South it was worse, according to the 'goddam radicals' spouting on soap boxes in Union Square, New York's 'Speakers' Corner'. There, it was peonage, a longer day than mine for $2 a day, slaving among the cotton gins of Gastonia. Feelings of social injustice stirred within me deeper than any I had experienced before. I also began to understand why it was possible to buy a well-made pure cotton shirt for less than 90 cents.

I developed a new taste in literature: I read Mike Gold in the Marxist magazine, 'New Masses' and the novelist John Dos Passos; I chuckled at Gropper's savage cartoons. I pored appreciatively over back numbers of Mencken's 'American Mercury' in the reference library.

My day began at 6.30 in the morning. After I had washed, shaved and dressed I had breakfast at a lunch wagon by Sutter Avenue. A cereal, an egg sandwich and two large cups of coffee (all for 25 cents). Then Harry and I boarded the subway train. A nickel apiece (tuppence ha'penny) took us both into town, where our paths diverged.

I clocked in at 8 a.m. when I was handed my first batch of telegrams for delivery to the big brokerage houses fringing the Wall Street Stock Exchange. That was the official bourse. Across the road, round Liberty Street, was the unofficial Stock Exchange, known as The Kerb, where hucksters sold their shares literally on the sidewalk. These shares were as good (or bad) as the ones dealt with on the Stock Exchange proper, under the aegis of the Securities Exchange Commission, but they represented cash flotations too small to make handling by the big brokers worthwhile.

The Stock Exchange mandarins occupied some pretty fancy office suites. Delivering telegrams, I would occasionally wander into magnificent, inch-deep carpeted board rooms. A couple of dozen investors would be sitting around on easy chairs watching the fluctuations in their shares being registered on a huge board. It stretched across an entire wall, with a clerk continually amending the figures to accord with minute by minute dealings on the floor of the Exchange.

Indoor speculation wasn't entirely confined to such salubrious surroundings. I was shooting pool in a sleazy billiard hall on 9th Avenue and 27th Street with a shrimp of an Italian who wheeled racks of coats and dresses around the wholesale houses, when the tape machine in the corner started chattering. My 30 cents an hour fellow member of the lumpen proletariat held his cue suspended in the air for a moment listening carefully. Then he placed the cue gently on the green baize and joined a little knot of men already fingering the tape as it spilled from the ticker. When the machine just as abruptly stopped, Dino returned to the table and picked up his cue with a satisfied smirk. "I'm doing all right," he said. He was playing margins. For $200 down, his life savings, Dino had first option on stocks valued at $2,000. If the shares went up, the value of his marginal holding increased: if the traffic went the other way, he had to make good the deficit to retain his 10 per cent interest. But in 1929, despite the growing number of people out of work, ignored as being due purely to what the papers called 'technological redeployment', stocks never went down. It was always up, up. They reached a plateau, where they stayed for a while, then up they went again.

Working on Wall Street, I took a great interest in the game. A gambler myself, I was fascinated by this craze for Stock Exchange speculation, which seemed to affect everyone in the city with a couple of bucks to spare. Candidly, if I'd had anything of a bankroll I would have taken a flyer myself. It would have been relatively easy to get in, make a killing and get out quick. But I knew my Samuel Berkovitz: he would go for the big odds *schtummers* and stay in long enough to get his balls chewed off like most of the rest.

But I would still have been different from the other gamblers in that I knew from my reading and Union Square listening that the whole shabby business was a bubble liable to burst at any moment. I studied the financial columns in the papers. I noted the increasing pluses and only the rare occasional minuses, but I also read the ominous signs of dropping freight car loadings nationwide.

I spoke as knowledgeably as any bucket shop proprietor of portfolios, convertibles, trusts, debentures and mutual funds. I wasn't a bit put out by the robbery, jobbery, scheming and chicanery which went on all around me. By birth and upbringing, I was and remain a natural sceptic – except for horse racing, when my faith is positively messianically religious. Later that year when the crash came, I wasn't surprised to find the portfolios full of nothing but air and water. Mutual funds with no funds, mutual only in their misery, and so-called trusts, proving to be utterly untrustworthy.

That was some months in the future, however. The Wall Street bully boys were still riding the crest of the wave when Myer Goldblatt came into my life and I cast anchor alongside my natural habitat, an East Side trouser makers' workshop.

Chapter 10

The ad said simply: 'Wanted: pants cutter – fixer for East Side loft.' There was a telephone number. It was still before 8 in the morning when I rang up. A voice gave me the address and told me to come along to Suffolk Street for an interview.

"When?" I asked.

"Now. Can you come now?"

"Sure," I said.

"Well, come."

I had casually picked up a discarded 'World' on the subway *on route* to my Wall Street office and the ad caught my eye by chance. It stood out from the uniform mass of grey matter while I was leafing through the paper looking for something interesting on the sports pages. As there was only the most tenuous connection between Western Union and myself, nobody would be deeply distressed if I delayed my appearance on Wall Street for an hour or two, or even if I didn't show up at all. Devoid of any guilt feelings about dereliction of duty, I altered my course for Suffolk Street.

The workshop itself was on the first floor of a shabby but solid old building. It was much as I had imagined it might be; a large oblong room hazy with a fug of tobacco smoke. Steam from the pressing irons turned the naked white electric bulbs hanging above the machines and tables into jaundiced yellow blobs, with a halo round the edges.

The owner of the voice on the phone was hardly what I had expected. He turned out to be a short, compactly built Jew in his late fifties with a neatly trimmed beard and bright eyes, wearing the orthodox black satin skull cap. I had coupled the cool American telephone voice with the persona of a smart, clean-shaven, up-to-date Yankee Doodle Dandy.

Bent over their machines, shirt sleeves hitched up with elastic bands, the tassels of ritual *tsitsis* – cut down praying shawls – dangling beneath their unbuttoned waistcoats, were two other bearded, skull-capped Jews. At the pressing tables stood two more burly, bearded men similarly dressed.

They looked up for a moment to give me a cursory glance, then bent back to their tasks.

"Sam Berkovitz," I said above the whirr of the machines.

"Myer Goldblatt," the voice answered. "Shalom." We shook hands.

"You can cut?" I nodded.

"And fix?"

"Yes." I said.

"Experienced?"

"Since I left school. In my father's workshop. In London. On my own and as a journeyman." Goldblatt smiled approvingly. But I wasn't quite sure. I gestured towards the bearded men. "I must tell you now, Mr. Goldblatt, I don't go to *shul*. I'm not *frum*. I'm not an observant Jew at all."

"Who's asking you?" he said. "So long as you can cut and fix."

"I can do that," I assured him. "As good as anyone in the trade."

"Okay," ge said. "I'm *frum*, but I can't cut and fix. You cut and fix but you are not *frum*. So, together we make a *frum* cutter and fixer. Right?"

"If it's okay with you," I said, "fine."

"So long as you are not bringing bacon and eggs into the workshop, or trying to *yentz shicksahs* on my cutting table. What you are doing outside is not my business. We all are talking mostly Yiddish here. *Radst Yiddish?*"

"*A bistle*"' I said. "Not much. But I understand. *Ich fershteh zehr gut.*"

I took my coat off and started work. By lunch break I convinced Goldblatt of my skill as a tradesman. The job was mine for $22 a week.

In 1929, prohibition in New York was a farce. Sometimes with tragic overtones. Everybody who wanted a drink or needed a drink, drank. The tragedies occurred when bathroom hooch collected some of the utensil's enamel or other impurities, which turned the liquid toxic and killed or blinded the drinkers. One of the tabloids printed a clock on the back page marking off by minute and hour hands the day's fatalities. First from automobiles, followed by homicide. Bad booze always came a close third.

The pressers, although orthodox, were a couple of toughies from Odessa. They were powerful men, strong as bullocks. Apart from work, *shul* and their children, they had no other interests. They had little concern for what was happening on the European continent. All they knew about Britain was that it was created by Disraeli and owned by Rothschild. But they did have a sense of humour. They'd been Bundists in their youth and were now lapsed atheists with a taste for the hard stuff. Waiting for the machinists to run up seams or pockets, the pressers would drop into the speakeasy across the street and stay until Myer hung an American flag out of the window. Old Glory meant there was now plenty of work for them to get on with.

If the machine operators were way, way behind their work, the pressers would troop off to another popular 'blind pig' in Essex Street. I liked that. It gave me an opportunity to slip out for an extra breath of fresh air while I made an unnecessary detour before gathering them back into the fold. This joint was close to Essex Market Court, and supposed to be on the site of Charlie Smith's (born Solly Solomon) famous Silver Dollar Saloon, which, in the days when liquor was legal, boasted a floor paved from wall to wall with silver dollars. I joined my pressers there for a drink, once. But only once. I paid 25 cents for a shot and it tasted like barbed wire.

Goldblatt's loft had a very congenial atmosphere. There was never a dull moment. The pressers were always singing Yiddish songs from the latest Goldfaden operetta or cracking bawdy jokes. We worked a five-day week, finishing on winter Fridays well before sunset, so that Goldblatt and his flock could attend *erev Shabbat* service at the local synagogue. Every week day, work was suspended for half an hour or so in the late afternoon for the evening service, which was held in the loft. For this, where a *minyan* (quorum of ten adult male Jews) was required, usually half a dozen or so workmen came down from the upstairs lofts to participate. If they were one short, it was understood that I was perfectly willing to make up the *minyan* provided I was not required to pray, merely to be there.

Scissors were put aside, irons were couched in the rest, electric power switched off. The gamey workshop ambience vanished and faces became serious as the men donned their praying shawls, swaying and muttering responses in unison, looking East, like Rembrandt's old Amsterdam Jews, towards the Temple in Jerusalem.

All week I lived frugally. My daily diet rarely varied and never cost more than a dollar. For breakfast I had a cereal, egg sandwich and a crusty roll washed down with a couple of cups of coffee. My mid-day meal was some form of egg dish, an omelette or egg and chips, with usually a raw onion and a large hard tomato. Dinner in the evening, my main meal, cost around 30 cents. (Again, that figure! It always seemed to loom large in my life.) Dinner comprised a large bowl of vegetable soup, another eggs and chips, fruit salad and cream with as much rye bread as I could eat for nothing.

On Thursdays, Harry and I dined at a delicatessen on Christie Street. We entered the restaurant in the same reverent spirit that drew Goldblatt and company to *shul*. Our taste buds were immediately titillated by ad lib offerings of sauerkraut, olives and pickled cucumbers displayed on the table. For *hors d'oeuvres* – a meal in itself – we had enormous portions of chopped herring, chopped liver or a mixture of highly seasoned chopped eggs and onions. Then came lokshen soup and wurst, or roast chicken with stuffed neck and French fries, followed by fresh fruit or a fruit salad. White coffee was out because the delicatessen was strictly kosher, and anything with milk in it after a meat main course was forbidden according to halachic law. We had tea with lemon instead. The bill for each of us was 95 cents and for the other 5 cents I bought the biggest cigar in the place and smoked till my stomach felt settled enough for me to stagger from the table and walk home.

What made Goldblatt's particularly attractive was that, apart from a five-day week, a rarity among small workshops even in America and utterly unknown in England in the '20s, I could get out of the loft twice a day on official business, as it were. I toured the Canal Street shops in the morning for orders and took the almost completed garments to the finishers in the afternoon. We had three of them, all Italian housewives who lived in Columbia Street on the Lower East Side, a part of Little Italy noted for its shooting affrays. "Duck if you are hearing any firing", Goldblatt warned me, only half in earnest, "but don't be alarmed, it is nothing personal."

The women behaved exactly like Mrs Goldblatt on the one occasion I visited Myer's home, or Solly's aunt. They pressed mountains of pizzas and lasagna upon me as if I hadn't eaten for years. There was some shooting there – I read about it in the papers – but it never happened when I was around. Some of it was domestic feuding, but most was between local Mafiosi fighting for control of the area. These gangsters were folk heroes. Our finishers had rafts of kids and all of them wanted to grow up like Al Capone, not the Pope. There was method in their badness. These youngsters were pragmatists. Already they had noticed that the only people around them with any money were hoodlums or those with gangster connections.

A happier feature of East Side life was potato pies. They cost a nickel. They were big and peppery and hot from the brazier. You could get them at nearly every street corner and they made a winter day's perambulating a pleasure.

There was a constant stream of visitors to the loft: shopkeepers, the occasional private customer, Italian felling hands bringing back work or their kids coming for more cottons and tape, and, of course, officials. The local Fire Chief came regularly to check up on fire hazards and to ensure the City Ordinances were observed. We knew when he was calling and since it was illegal in these lofts, we stopped smoking for half an hour beforehand. The stale odour of stogies was still so strong however, the Fire Chief would have had to have some serious olfactory blockage not to notice it. He would walk around the workshop, put his foot on the fire escape ladder and murmur 'Everything seems to be okay.' Casually, he would mention the Firemen's Ball and Goldblatt bought a few tickets. That concluded the inspection.

The Police Chief also dropped in to examine the burglar alarms and gratefully accepted a contribution to the Patrolmen's Widows Benevolent Fund. Goldblatt paid up like a gentleman. For him, these bribes were facts of workshop life, a necessary evil, like insurance.

Around election time, people came to the loft who, for a change, wanted to do things for us. Both Republican ward bosses and Tammany Hall Democratic big shots gave away cheap cigars, made promises they never intended to keep and stayed long enough to crack some bad jokes in Yiddish with a strong Irish accent.

Goldblatt's two sons, both in their late twenties, occasionally visited our loft, the younger one Maxie more frequently than Jules, the elder. Maxie was an earnest, cultured young man, a graduate of the Juilliard Academy. New York had nothing much to offer him in the serious music line. He played the fiddle on odd gigs round town, for bar mitzvahs and engagement parties and, in summer was a band-leader/host at Grossinger's, a small, kosher, Jewish holiday camp recently opened in the Catskills, the 'borscht belt.'

Maxie was married. His wife, an experienced secretary, worked in an uptown office. Between them they drew in quite a handsome income and as they lived modestly in a small East Side cold water flat, they were able to put by a considerable sum over the years. Maxie invested their savings in first mortgages on houses and other real estate. He was as sceptical as I was about the Stock Exchange, unlike brother Jules, a doctor who gave up medicine altogether for speculation, at which he was phenomenally successful.

Whatever stock Jules touched shot up like a rocket. He'd come in loaded down with largesse. A couple of bottles of uncut liquor for the pressers, cigarettes for the machinists, something for the old man and for me, half a dozen gigantic Henry Clay Havana cigars. One day, he showed us, not cockily but with a certain pride of achievement, a cheque for $200,000. Profits from a single day's trading, he said.

Old man Goldblatt wasn't impressed. "It's only paper," he said. "You are only buying more paper with it. Why are you not getting out while the going's good and buying something substantial? Real estate like Maxie." Jules grinned. The old man was always giving him good advice. Like get married, for example. He would, one day; meantime he was playing the field. He had a Duplex apartment on Riverside Drive and was getting mentions in the newspapers by Winchell and Sobell about squiring starlets at Broadway openings. He was even pictured in the gravures, the handsome young doctor, the Wall Street whizz kid, always with a dazzling broad hanging on his arm. It was the elusive first million Jules was after. Once that was in the bag he'd quit.

Although we shared a room, I didn't see too much of Harry Singer. We had breakfast and travelled to work together and met Thursday nights at the delicatessen on Christie Street. Occasionally, on Sunday mornings we walked down Sutter Avenue, or by the car barns in Utica, looking for a flutter on the dice. We usually located a floating crap game run by one Jersey Slim, the archetypal Reliable Nathan. Though Slim's clients rarely ventured more than half a dollar a bet, Slim's modus vivendi was simple. He produced a couple of dozen dice from his capacious coat pockets and as they pattered on the ground he invited the whole world to participate at 5 cents a throw. Anyone could win a fortune. Himself, he stood aloof. He was a business man not a gambler. Apart from collecting nickels, Jersey Slim had no further interest in the game.

Harry and I also visited the movies when some much-touted talkie was on, but he spent most of his leisure time with his cousins and occasional girlfriends. Being a bit of a loner anyway, that suited me. With my brother Al in Britain, apart from Harry, I was happily alone in this big city.

Spring in New York is the finest season of the year. Even the air has a bounce and when it rains it falls like sparkling champagne. I loved the smell and the feel of the wet pavements under my feet on my twice-daily trips around town. But it doesn't last. With the heat and humidity comes summer, sliding imperceptibly into autumn and the darkness before winter.

The cold days found me still at Goldblatt's. Still running errands. Still a glorified shop boy. Meantime, what of the Cooper Union? It was still there, but I wasn't. I'd been to collect all the available bumpf and discovered that my electrical engineering degree was a three-year course. To take it I had to have some practical knowledge of the subject. A piece of cake, I thought. Wasn't I the bright boy at school – Taffy Wilson's white-haired wonder? Didn't I make a cat's whisker wireless receiving set myself all those years ago in London? Electricity, for anyone who bothered to take a walk by night down Broadway, was obviously the coming thing.

Journeymen electricians I met were already pulling in over a dollar an hour. An electrician with a degree, who could plan and design circuits, could write his own ticket on the labour market.

I went to the library and got a couple of books to punch up on the subject, but the most elementary primer shook me. I discovered I could just about remember Ohm's Law. I recalled something of the process of induction, but I'd quite forgotten the functions of transformers and condensers. I couldn't follow circuits all the way round. Signs I had been familiar with as a kid threw me.

I realised I was going to have some difficulty hoisting myself out of the gas age by my bootstraps, but I persevered, and gradually, slowly, I was getting the hang of things. Each chapter became less puzzling than the last, although I kept falling asleep over the text at night like my studious young medical friend Milton did over the switchboard years ago at Danny's.

In extenuation, I must point out that I was pretty fatigued. I'd worked a twelve-hour day standing at the cutting table and, between times, walked to Canal Street and the finishers. Saturdays, I was resting or listening in Union Square or tramping through Central Park and exploring the waterfront. Sunday wasn't even long enough to get through the newspapers. But in the New Year, I promised myself, I'd sign up with the Cooper Union and keep my nose to the grindstone come what may, till that precious parchment was in my pocket.

Chapter 11

Since my Wall Street engagement I'd got in the habit of watching closely the Stock Exchange quotations. They were listed on the back pages of the dailies. In September I began to note an odd phenomenon. The closing market prices were showing a considerable fluctuation. More and more minuses had begun to appear among the previously overwhelming pluses and, by October, had actually outstripped them. I suspected something very sinister was afoot. How bad it was came like a thunderbolt on October 29th when the financial news was promoted to the front pages. Huge banner headlines shrieked 'Market Breaks' in type normally reserved for cancelling the world series or announcing the second coming of Christ. In the next two weeks, stocks dropped 30 billion dollars and wiped out not only the little margin gamblers but also big privateers. Among them was the president of one Utilities conglomerate who, unhinged when his stock over that period slumped from 113 dollars 50 cents to 4 dollars, jumped from the ledge of a New York hotel and didn't live to see it sink even lower.

"Up till now there was in the whole world only one Wailing Wall – in Jerusalem," a New Yorker wit recorded sardonically, "but since October 29th every wall on Wall Street has become wet with speculators' tears."

Even Myer got in on the act. "Be careful" he cautioned me. "When you are going down Wall Street, walk in the road. On the sidewalk some stock jobber trying to balance his books is liable to be falling on your head."

Goldblatt was trying to make light of the disastrous financial situation, but he was really afraid for Jules. He hadn't seen him for weeks and was scared he'd been savaged in the debacle. Myer's foreboding was right. He unburdened himself in the workshop: "You know my son, the doctor. The millionaire. My Jules? Last night he is coming round to borrow money for petrol. Petrol! He is driving to Ohio. There is a big hospital there wants doctors. His Duplex apartment is gone. His Cadillac is gone. Everything. All he's got left is this banged-out jalopy he is picking up for a few dollars in some secondhand junk yard."

"I am cleaned out, Pop" he tells me. "Every cent."

"So you're finished with all that madness, that *meshugaas*."

"It is finished with me," he says. "I want to get as far away from Wall Street as this old tin can will carry me."

"You mean it?" I ask.

"By my mother's life," he is swearing. "I know you've got your own troubles, your *tsoores*, Dad, but lend me enough to get to Ohio. I am paying you back every cent, you'll see."

"Well," I say – "a *kapoorah*! To hell with the millions and the Cadillacs and the apartment and the smart, skinny, non-Jewish girl-friends (forbidden fruit). So long as you've got your health and strength and want to be a real *mensch* again. A healer. A doctor. Truthfully Jules, I am glad. Real glad."

"So, okay. You're glad. Now, can you lend me enough to hit the road, Pop?"

"Not so fast," I am telling him. You are all bushed out. First you are taking a vacation." He is looking at me as if I'm *meshuggah*."

"Vacation?"

"Vacation," I say. "Somewhere nice, like the Bahamas."
"Who's got money for vacations?" he says.

"You have," I say. And I am putting in his hand some diamond clips he buys my Becky when he makes some big killing. They must be worth at least a thousand dollars. And you'll never believe this, Sam. He is genuinely forgetting he ever gives her those things. Of course, he doesn't want to take them back. But I tell him his mother is never wearing the clips. Becky doesn't really like them. They are too young and flashy, but she is not wanting to hurt his feelings.

A couple of days later, as I was leaving the workshop, I ran into Maxie. His face was grey and drawn. He appeared to be stooping more than usual. He looked like someone sickening for a dread disease. He shook his head sadly when he met my eyes, and at once

I was sure I knew what was wrong. "It's Jules?," I guessed. "Something's up with Jules?"

Maxie's first words confirmed my suspicions. "You know what happened to Jules? Now it's happened to me. I'm wiped out. Ruined!" "But I thought – ," I started.

"Yes, I know," he snapped back at me. "All my money was tied up in real estate. Safe as houses. But my attorney was playing the market. He used my first mortgages as collateral. Bloody good job he shot himself or I'd have strangled the bastard with my own hands."

His violent tone turned to bitterness. "What chokes me is that Jules at least enjoyed himself with his paper money. Swam in champagne. Draped chorus girls with diamonds. Me, I wouldn't even buy my Linda a new coat. I had to convert every last cent we saved into bricks and mortar. Now what have I got? Like it says in the bible *'Ush und porech'* – dust and ashes. Not even a few happy memories."

The Depression was the great leveler. As it really began to bite, impartially it bled dry the Goldblatt brothers, my pool partner Dino, the postman, the liftman and the little shop keeper in his corner drugstore.

Harry Singer had sensed it coming early on. Along with his personal fastidiousness he was a canny, calculating character. Latterly he was employed at a furrier's, pulling in 40 bucks a week and more. Being a luxury trade, it felt the pinch first, and Harry, foreseeing the work petering out entirely, withdrew his 500-odd dollars savings from the bank, upped stakes and went home. In England, at least, being such an expert craftsman, he was always sure of some sort of a job.

Paradoxically, in the beginning, the Depression didn't affect Goldblatt's at all. On the contrary, business was booming. We were saved by the second pair of pants in a two-pants suit. The suits sold in Canal Street were jackets and trousers made up in bulk and shipped there from the factories, together with some extra bolts of cloth for each range. Customers buying suits had the option of purchasing an extra pair of pants of the same material made to measure ostensibly on the premises, and about half of them usually took advantage of the offer.

That was where Goldblatt's came in. We made the extra pants. With the deepening Depression, nobody bought new suits. They made do with the old ones and prettied them up with a pair of new trousers, which made sense since the original jackets almost always outlasted the pants.

New Year wasn't happy for anyone and as 1930 progressed, Goldblatt's began to wilt. People could no longer afford even a single new pair of pants. The number of orders coming in was not sufficient to keep his full operation ticking over. It was obvious Myer would soon be forced to trim his staff.

At least one presser and one machinist would have to go, and as a logical extension, me. But at least I was still working. Outside the loft, New York, that once proud bustling city, was plunged into gloom and utter misery. The place took on the hungry, shabby look of London. It only came to life on the streets where a soup kitchen was installed when, as if by magic, the word got round and breadlines formed, stretching right round the block.

Central Government, to its shame, abdicated all responsibility for even the minimal wellbeing of the citizens who had elected it. Civic leaders, expert at putting their hands in the public pockets, didn't want to know now that there was nothing left to pick and the survivors were expected to fend for themselves. Private charities did their best. The Salvation Army worked heroically. Some of the wealthy, old-money families like the Whitneys spent millions setting up their own charitable outlets, providing food parcels and even clothes. If one person in a family of five or six was working, they were lucky. All of them had to live on what the solitary breadwinner provided.

I felt almost embarrassed to be still in full employment, especially when I was buttonholed on the sidewalk for a handout by someone whose clothes still showed remnants of their former quality. I didn't gloat at their distress. Quite the contrary, I was sorry for them. I couldn't help feeling they'd had an extra raw deal. They didn't know what had hit them. They hadn't my resilience, born from a lifetime spent in social insecurity, that cushioned me against whatever economic disasters might befall.

The well-spoken, young man who begged unashamedly for a nickel or a dime made me revise my plans for the Cooper Union. Here were men with not one degree but probably a whole string, asking for a handout. What, I asked myself, was the point of putting myself in hock for three years just to bash my brains out to get a useless piece of parchment?

Soon the inevitable happened. Goldblatt said he had to let me go. My future in America seemed bleak. Now the Cooper Union no longer held any attraction, I didn't want to stay on. I decided to get out while I could still make it on my own.

My savings were in a Brooklyn branch of the Bank of the United States in Pitkin Avenue. A Jewish bank, the branch was a sort of family affair run on happy-go-lucky lines, employing everyone's aunt and uncle. The cashiers, all solid homely citizens, spoke Yiddish, Russian, Polish and sometimes English when required.

I presented myself at the cashier's grille and slid over a cheque for 350 dollars to close my account. He asked me to wait for a moment and called his brother-in-law the manager, who came out, greeted me cordially and led me into a glass partitioned little anteroom. "What's the matter, landsman?" he asked me. "Why are you taking out all your money? Is it something you've heard? If so, let me assure you the Bank of the United States is as solid as the Rock of Gibraltar." He threw out his hands in protest. "Now you're a smart Yiddisher boychik. You know we pay the highest rates of interest. Why take your *gelt* elsewhere? The Vanderbilts and Morgans have got enough. Why make the rich *goyim* richer?"

It took a little while, but I finally convinced him that I had nothing against the bank. I was genuinely going home. "In that case," he agreed reluctantly, "let me remind you that the bank has an agency for all the international shipping lines. We'll be glad to sell you a ticket without charging a cent extra commission."

At the time, me thought he did protest too much. I wasn't surprised therefore when, just a week prior to my departure for England, the Bank of the United States went broke and the Pitkin Avenue branch closed its doors.

The day before my ship was due to sail, I went for a last trip round New York. I started off as I had done every working morning, on the subway. As I came out of the tunnel on to Brooklyn Bridge and saw the whole downtown area stretched out before me, I felt the customary jolt of joyous appreciation, but today it was tinged with sadness. Tomorrow I would no longer be part of the scene.

It was a chilly day but I was in a warm, sentimental mood. With a few hundred bucks in my pocket I was ripe for a touch. As I slouched along, I gradually got rid of all the loose coins in my pockets without even bothering to notice who took them from me.

On 27th Street, a hand gently touched my arm. A voice said, "Got a dime for a cup of coffee, sport?" Too late, buddy, I thought. I turned towards a shortish, shabbily dressed man in a long threadbare coat wearing a flat cap. Two weeks' rough growth of beard shadowed his face, but I recognized him immediately. In a city of six million strangers, Danny. And no more than a hundred yards from where we'd first met three years ago.

"Danny!" I said. "It's Sam. Sam Berkovitz. I worked for you. Remember?" "Sam?," he said dully. He looked hard then seemed to recognize me.

"Yes, Sam."

"Sorry. I didn't know it was you – how you doing Sam?"

"Not too bad," I told him. "It's my last day in New York. Got my steamship ticket. Sailing for England tomorrow. What's been happening to you, Danny? Caught short on the market? So, welcome to the club!" "You too?" he asked. "Well, only in a manner of speaking," I said. "If I didn't take a tumble it's only because I didn't have any money to lose."

"I did," Danny mumbled. "One hell of a lot." Now he spoke angrily. "Six months ago I could have sold out for a quarter of a million. Now I'm left *mitten tochas in droissen* – with my bare arse on the street."

It was useless trying to console him, but somehow I felt I owed Danny something. I groped for the bankroll in my pocket, slipped off a five-dollar bill and shoved it in his fist. He held the *finif* in a trembling hand and looked up at me mournfully, his head shaking as if he was suffering from Parkinson's. A fat tear oozed out of the corner of his eye, slid down the side of his nose and flattened softly on the banknote.

"I owe you that, for old time's sake." I said. "For giving me good advice. For telling me I needed more get up and go. Well, now I've got up and I'm going."

"God bless you, Sam," Danny muttered. I could hardly hear him. *"Gay gezunt –* go in good health. I wish I was going back home with you. This is a terrible country, so it is!"

Part 3

Back In The East End

Chapter 12

A couple of weeks after my return from America I had found my feet again in London and it was as though I'd never been away. I rented a room in Bedford Street at seven shillings a week, resumed my horse and dog betting schedule with Hymie and slipped effortlessly into the club, street corner and dole routine.

But it wasn't the old Sam. I'd returned with an extra dimension, a social conscience. I couldn't forget and, to this day, still remember with horror the sidewalk on 2nd Avenue, black with thousands of starving New Yorkers patiently queuing for a cup of coffee and a stale doughnut or a cheese sandwich.

The new Sam Berkovitz fitted in well with Stepney's street corner sub-culture, which had also undergone a subtle change in the couple of years I'd been away. America as a subject for discussion among youngsters was no longer top of the pops. It was now a place to dream about getting away from, not going to. With Mussolini in Italy, the rise of Hitler in Germany and the Mosley menace threatening us at home, fascism, after sport and girls, was our main preoccupation.

London in the '30s had at least this to commend it. We could, unlike in America, draw on some organised state assistance. As a single person, I got seventeen shillings a week unemployment benefit, until Ramsey Macdonald's National Government cut it to fifteen shillings and fivepence. That was in line with the employers' general attack on our living standards. In this connection, what's difficult for workers today to understand is that our struggles were not for more wages, but to resist cuts on the pittance we'd already won.

Work in my trade was seasonal. I was never employed for more than six months in the year, when my pay averaged £3.10s a week. For the other six months I drew the dole.

My first job back in England was with a firm named Mortimer's. They made a complete threepiece suit, trousers, jacket and waistcoat, for thirty-seven shillings and sixpence. Of course, it couldn't last, and by the end of 1931 they went broke. Me too. Only with me, being without funds was simply a return to the status quo. But I had enough stamps on my insurance card to qualify for the dole. That was the pattern of my life for the next few years; a job or jobs then the dole and in between, if necessary, the Unemployment Assistance Board (UAB).

After 26 weeks of drawing unemployment benefit, a claimant was no longer eligible for the dole but had to apply for UAB benefit, involving the universally hated Means Test. The Borough Council sent a Relieving Officer to investigate and he could query the claim if he didn't like the applicant's face or attitude, or saw an old gramophone on the sideboard with one new record – an obvious indication of vast hidden means. The Borough Council would then haul the claimant before a Court of Referees and confront him with the Relieving Officer's report. Once the Referees reached a decision, grudgingly over-riding their conviction that every applicant was a scrounger or a thief or more likely both, the benefit was paid through the Labour Exchange.

With two trips to America under my belt, I held forth as an acknowledged authority on the decline of the West, my arguments reinforced by liberal quotations from such as Spengler, culled from my omnivorous reading in the reference library. My regular diet was the Greyhound Express and the 4th Star, the horse racing edition, but I also read Kant, Schopenhauer, my favourite military historians Klausewitz and Liddell Hart, Kirkegaarde, Nietsche, Engels and even Karl Marx in small doses. I became a street corner oracle voicing instant, often contradictory judgements, at the drop of a cap. Way out ideas tumbled around my head and spilled unchecked from the tip of my tongue, until Nat Cohen came along. He acted as a catalyst, offering a cure for my mental indigestion.

Until Nat, I had a vague leftish stance. He polarised my attitude into a definite commitment to membership of the Communist Party. Nat became my guru. His teaching encouraged me to use Dialectical Materialism as an all-embracing philosophy. Nat himself applied it as a touchstone to the normal traffic of daily life. He shoved everything, including his breakfast, through the mincer of Dialectical Materialism. Right from the start, I was never anything like so doctrinaire. I found Dialectical Materialism merely a useful tool for certain mental evaluation and not a universal panacea.

Nat had only just returned to England from South America where he had lived for seven or eight years. Deported from Argentina as an illegal immigrant, but really because of his notoriety as a trades union organiser, his ship was shunted from port to port in Europe like a yo-yo. Nobody would have him. Finally, he landed in England, which didn't want Nat either, but had to accept him because he was London born. Immediately, he immersed himself in political activity and, when I met him, was firmly entrenched as Secretary of our local branch of the Communist Party.

Nat was a tailor's machinist, shorter than me and a few years older, but still on the right side of thirty. He had powerful shoulders, a big nose and small grey eyes that bit into you. When you spoke to him, he seemed to be listening to what was at the back of your words and making the inevitable Marxist connection.

"I don't care where you are or what you do," he constantly impressed upon me. "As a Communist, you make yourself a centre of influence. Always, you speak for and represent the Party." Nat was the type of disciplined, dedicated Communist who would accept without question anything that bore the imprimatur of the Party's Central Committee. If it was a party decision for him to cut off his right hand he would have submitted without demur. If he'd been Jonah and the Party told him to, he'd have swallowed the whale. He scorned the intolerance of orthodox society, yet was himself just as intolerant. Ready to sacrifice himself for the cause he believed in, he would quite happily, despite their objections, sacrifice everyone else as well.

Like Philby, Maclean, Burgess and Blunt, Nat's loyalty was supranational. He owed allegiance to no country but the workers of the world, as represented by the Soviet Union. Had he been in a position to do so, he'd have passed over secrets with the best of the Cambridge bunch. He was always disappearing on trips to Moscow as a member of fraternal delegations of trades unionists for courses at the Lenin Institute. I wouldn't be a bit surprised if he didn't also do a couple of little jobs for the KGB on the side.

Had Nat lived in fifteenth-century Spain, he'd certainly have been a familiar target of the Inquisition. No *auto da fé* would have been complete without him. If there was a heaven, and he got there,

Nat's first job after booking in with St Peter would be to form a Party cell. Slogans would suddenly appear on the Pearly Gates: 'Heaven is not enough.' 'Why should He have all the power?' 'We demand bigger halos.' 'Angels want larger wings.' Conversely, evidence of Nat's sojourn in the nether regions would soon be visible in flaming precepts like 'Devils demand hotter fires.'

I discovered later that Nat had a dossier on me, starting the day after our very first meeting. He showed me a big file he had completed over the years with a dossier for each member past and present of our St George's cell. I kidded him into giving me a glimpse of mine and discovered he'd assessed my character with amazing clarity in very few words: 'Has anarchistic tendencies, hobnobs with gamblers and other anti-social elements. Is lazy, undisciplined and cynical.' I couldn't agree more.

After the second World War, Nat left the Communist Party for a short period, due to a silly doctrinal dispute, while I was still an active member. By mutual consent, he kept well out of everyone's way, but I'd have been only too happy to pass the time of day with him when we bumped into each other in the street. Not so, Nat. He shied from me like a snorting thoroughbred. "Don't talk to me Sam," he warned. "You know I've been expelled from the Party. You're a member in good standing. You mustn't be seen fraternising with me. It's a matter of discipline. Don't blot your copybook. You're consorting with someone the Party's dubbed a deviationist – Goodbye!" He turned tail and fled. I looked back at him and thought – what on earth could you do with such people?

Chapter 13

That incident occurred, as far as I can remember, some time in 1950. In the '30s however, Nat, by virtue of his first-hand knowledge of revolutionary tactics abroad, was unquestioned leader of our group in Stepney. In fact, he was rapidly becoming a local folk hero. In the summer of 1936, he was cycling through Spain with a friend to join a workers' sports festival - the Spartakiad in Barcelona - when the Civil War erupted. Nat immediately joined the Government forces and soon became a section leader in the Thaelmann Centuria, the precursor of the International Brigade fighting in Spain. During the civil war, Nat was wounded when a bullet shattered his knee. He fell in love with a Spanish nurse, Ramona. When he was repatriated after Franco's victory, Cohen managed to smuggle her out with him to Paris. To get Ramona into Britain, he contacted his East End comrade-in-arms, Joe Jacobs and his wife, Pearl. They journeyed to France and met up with Nat and Ramona. Pearl then returned to Britain posing as a day tripper, while Cohen's future wife arrived in her new homeland using Pearl's passport.

The Party in Stepney was also undergoing upheavals during that fateful summer and autumn of 1936 and we sorely needed the advice of our absent elder statesman, Nat. The primary reason for our disarray was an inability to agree on the correct way to meet the growing menace of Mosely's fascists. The Party line according to the Central Committee insisted on us devoting the bulk of our energies to supporting the struggle against Franco in Spain. However, combating the rise of fascism in our own streets was regarded as important as well, though nevertheless more of a side issue.

Although some of the members agreed, others felt the emphasis was the wrong way round. The Communist Party had set in motion plans for a tremendous Save Spain Rally in Trafalgar Square on October 4th. Two weeks before the event, Mosley suddenly announced the same date for his own march through Stepney. It was a shrewd move that caught the Party off balance. We were obsessed by the Spanish Civil War, then in its third month, and most of our agitation and propaganda was directed towards aiding the loyalists. We had already distributed thousands of leaflets around the East End, calling for a maximum turnout in Trafalgar Square. Our squads had whitewashed miles of pavements and hoardings with slogans. 'No Paseran', the Spanish loyalist slogan 'They Shall Not Pass', appeared everywhere, alongside 'All Out Trafalgar Square October 4th'. Similar exhortations were splashed over pavements throughout the working-class areas of London. It was the most intensive campaign the London District Committee of the Communist Party had ever mounted and it showed every sign of evoking a tremendous response.

Desperate efforts were made through local authorities, the churches, the Home Office and other official channels to make the police ban Mosley's march altogether or force him to change his route. All to no avail. On the Monday before the date set for the march, the ten strong St George's cell held their regular weekly meeting at Fred's Café in Manningtree Street near Gardiner's Corner. Joe Jacobs, in Nat's absence our Secretary, was in the Chair. He was a burly young man with one glass eye, a garment presser about twenty or twenty-one years old, the youngest member of our group. Joe didn't beat about the bush. "Comrades," he said. "We must make a decision right now. I propose we suspend all other business and discuss what we're going to do about Mosley.

Seconded?"

A nod from me.

"Any objections?"

Not a single hand was raised against.

"So moved," said Joe.

We argued until midnight and finally agreed that local Party members would have to stand firm in Stepney and resist Mosley by force, if necessary. Joe was delegated to present our case the following day to the London District Committee at the Centre in King Street. His main brief was to press for a change of venue - to switch from Trafalgar Square to a rally in Stepney instead.

To our dismay, the London District Committee wouldn't hear of it. Among them were the shrewdest political brains in Britain, some of whom had served prison terms for their beliefs. They pointed out that the Party's maximum effort had to be directed towards saving Spain. We were at a crossroads in the future path of Europe, perhaps of the world. Democracy was in danger. Hitler was rampant. The place to stop him was in Spain, not Stepney. And the way to stop him was to force the government to give aid and succour to the loyalists. Joe wasn't convinced and said so.

The 'Save Spain' rally could take place a little later. The Mosley danger was right here and now. On our streets. This was Sunday. The people in the East End were looking to us for a lead. They had come to rely on the Party. In our propaganda, in our literature and selling and door-to-door collections, we had hammered home: Trust us. Support us. We are on your side. We'll protect you.

If we weren't there on October 4th we'd be letting them down. We'd be letting the Party down too. It would destroy the political power base we'd built up locally over the past ten years. Joe's answer from the Centre, however, was still 'No'. The Rally in Trafalgar Square stood.

Next morning, we received by hand an official memorandum from the Centre:

'The London District Committee has made the following arrangements regarding Mosley's march:

1) A Party meeting to take place at Salmon and Ball pub in Bethnal Green. Another meeting in Piggott Street in Poplar. i.e. near to each end of the march. These two meetings will be kept orderly and under control. Avoid clashes.

2) Loudspeaker vans will tour the area advertising the meetings.

3) Thousands of leaflets are waiting at Carter's Bookshop for immediate distribution.

4) The Stepney comrades must rally masses to each of these meetings. Mostly to Salmon and Ball.

5) Keep order. Give no excuse for the government to say we, like the British Union of Fascists, are a bunch of hooligans. If Mosley decides to march, let him. Don't attempt disorder. The time is too short to get a 'They Shall Not Pass' policy across. It would only be a harmful stunt.

6) See there's a good strong meeting at each end of the march. Push the Party's leaflets round the crowds. Our biggest trouble on the night will be to keep order and discipline.'

We were horrified. To us this was plain surrender. We turned the directive down flat. Feverishly we canvassed other Stepney wards and found they were with us one hundred percent.

On Wednesday, Joe was despatched to King Street again, this time to approach the Central Committee armed with motions, resolutions and petitions representing the whole spectrum of Stepney's population and to deliver what was virtually an ultimatum: back us officially. Change the Trafalgar Square date or we act independently of the Centre.

Such defiance of the highest authority was unheard of in Party annals. It was an agonising decision for us to make as we prided ourselves on discipline being our real strength. But it worked. Joe got his way and returned at midnight with the news that the Central Committee had agreed to our demands. They had not fully appreciated, they said, the deep feelings aroused in the East End by the proposed march. They would cancel the Trafalgar Square Rally and support completely the 'Stop Mosley' call.

There wasn't any time for jubilation. We had to descend on the pavements with our pots and our brushes and scrub out the old assembly point and paint in the new venue, Gardiner's Corner. The logistics of the switch were horrendous. We were debarred from all means of mass communication, apart from loudspeaker vans. All the national newspapers were against us. The Labour Party's 'Daily Herald' would have nothing to do with us, and even our own 'Daily Worker' only decided to support us the day after Joe's 'or else' visit to the Centre.

We worked like demons; Joe hardly slept at all. When his fever subsided for a brief spell, he would seem utterly depressed. At such moments, he would ask me: "Am I doing right, Sam? What do you think Nat would have done?"

I did my best to reassure him, but I could understand his anxiety. He was on a hiding to nothing. He had openly defied a Party directive, and that would always be held against him. If only twenty or thirty thousand demonstrators showed up and Mosley marched, King Street would crow: 'We told you so – the time was too short.' But if, as our hasty canvas indicated, the crowds could be up to ten times as great, three or four hundred thousand, that would bring Joe another set of problems – how to control the lunatic fringe. They might spearhead wild rushes, swamping the police and the fascists, then march up to the West End themselves, smashing windows, burning and looting. They would create a revolutionary situation without having the organisation to take advantage of it and the government's backlash would probably wipe out all our hard-won political gains.

In the event, Joe needn't have worried. About a quarter of a million demonstrators showed up at Gardiner's Corner representing anti-fascist groups from all over London, with the Jewish population and the dockers being prominent. They choked every possible line of Mosley's march, armed themselves and threatened violence if the march took place. The Chief Police Commissioner himself, Sir Philip Game, told a hemmed-in Moseley he couldn't proceed and the fascist march was abandoned. It was a glorious victory. You could hear the cheering as far east as the Blackwall Tunnel.

Chapter 14

The traumatic events of October 4th may have finished Moseley's British Union as a mass movement in the East End, but fascism on the Continent advanced apace, and I watched with growing apprehension our doomed decade sliding inexorably towards Armageddon. That's the Olympian view. Down to earth, however, my life for the next couple of years continued much as before. The Party occupied only two or three evenings a week. There was the mandatory weekly Cell meeting, barely reaching an attendance of double figures and the large monthly Branch meeting two to three hundred strong which, guided by a luminary from King Street, laid down the broad policy line as determined by the Central Committee.

I managed to find time to visit a Music Hall at least once a week with Hymie and go most evenings for long walks with him around the City and West End. And, of course, I continued to study form pursuant to my career as a fancier of horseflesh.

Hymie was a treasure. More, he was my treasurer. He had an uncanny knack of picking winners and spotting likely results on the short list football pools and greyhound tracks. Although my own forays in the field ended mainly in disaster, I could usually count on Hymie to come up with a short-odds win double or a place treble to keep me level pegging. I wasn't the only one. Half of Bedford Street relied on him to augment their meagre incomes. When he was on form, Hymie was a vital part of the Street's domestic economy. It got so that I would borrow a few shillings from him at the beginning of the week and confidently tell him to take it off my winnings on Saturday. We seemed to be lucky for each other. A couple of times while I was in the States, he wrote he wasn't doing too well with the horses. I sent him a dollar for luck and a few weeks later I got a pound in the mail, four times as much as I'd sent. On another occasion I got back three pounds for my dollar.

For me, 1938 was a watershed. I met Bessie Cohen. She was in her early twenties, about ten years my junior. She came into Fred's Café one evening with a girlfriend whom I knew slightly. On being introduced I was immediately bowled over. Bessie was tall, much taller than the average young Jewish girl in our neighbourhood, and with her long black hair, blazing dark eyes and magnificent figure, she looked like a Gipsy Princess. Today, nearly fifty years on, and quite grey, she looks, with her classic features still sharply etched, like a Dowager Empress should look.

After we'd been going out together for a bit, I nearly lost her. Besotted by the depth of my feelings, late one night I used up the whitewash for two mass meetings in a long unbroken line across the pavement leading to her front door, and embellished it with a big heart pierced by an arrow and the letters 'S Loves B'. In the morning, her mother told me she was furious. At the shop where she worked, the girls wouldn't stop taking the mickey. I managed to convince Bess, however, that my intentions were serious and since I had just landed a regular job, we became engaged. A couple of months later we got married and moved into a tiny flat above a garage in Cannon Street Road, a turning off Commercial Road, which I still occupy 50 years later and where, in 1939, our son Barry was born.

Part 4

The War

Chapter 15

Britain declared War on Sunday, September 3rd, 1939. On Monday, September 4th, Harry Pollitt, writing in the 'Daily Worker', the official organ of the Communist Party, declared: 'This is the most just war in history and should be fully supported.' On Tuesday, September 5th, the Daily Worker's 'Just War' changed overnight into 'Just another Imperialist war, a betrayal of the Working Class', a war which they advised the workers to oppose with all their might.

Apparently, the full implication of Stalin's deal with Hitler, whereby Uncle Joe would be allowed to annexe Eastern Poland in exchange for allowing Adolf a free hand in the West, took longer than expected to filter through to the Party's top brass in Britain. Understandably a lot of the comrades were confused by this sudden reversal of policy, and of course heads had to roll. Harry Pollitt, a likeable ex-boilermaker, had to issue a public recantation in print to the effect that he had made a lamentable error of judgement and was therefore no longer fit to be Secretary of the Communist Party of Great Britain. In Uncle Joe's Russia, Harry's head would have rolled for real; here, Pollitt merely resigned and was later rehabilitated.

I didn't go for those just/unjust contortions myself. I felt the war against Hitler was entirely justified. I still believe it was absolutely necessary to destroy fascism before we would be able to build a civilised society. 'Stop Hitler' was a message I and my comrades had hammered home from a thousand street corner platforms and for me it was still valid. It was my war, and as soon as my wife and son were settled, I would be in it up to the hilt.

This was the beginning of the so-called 'phoney war', but for me the battle for survival was very real. All the clothing factories in the East End closed down the moment war was declared. Bessie and our boy were evacuated to Aylesbury. Left in London, I had no wife, no kid, no money and no flat. I was turned out because the garage above which I lived was requisitioned for ambulances and our rooms taken over for ambulance personnel. Fortunately, I was able to move in with Hymie, whose mother and sisters had gone to stay with relatives in Wales. Now I at least had a roof over my head, enough to eat and a few shillings when I wanted it. With Hymie, I lounged about town watching the sandbags piling up against official walls and various other civil defence activities, none of which brought the war home to me as much as the sudden silence of the childless East End streets. The very air seemed to be stagnant with no screeching youngsters to shake it about.

Leafing through a copy of the 'Tailor and Cutter' in the Whitechapel reference library, I noticed that a clothing firm in Bishop Auckland, way up in the north-east, was advertising for a uniforms trousers foreman. I thought, what the hell, even if it is in the wilderness, it's better to work there for a while than kick my heels doing nothing in London. I wrote to them right away offering my services and mentioning in particular my experiences of trousers manufacturing in America. I got a reply a couple of days later, fixing a weekend appointment and enclosing a return railway ticket.

I went up to Bishop Auckland on the Saturday and had a long session with the Greens, father and son, who owned the firm. I demonstrated my skill in grading patterns and my familiarity with the mechanised cutting knives, still fairly new here but old hat in the States. I talked real big as well, but I think what finally convinced them of my suitability was that, through trade connections, the son knew of my younger brother Solly, who was now a foreman at Simon Ackerman's in Crewe, which produced the Chester Barrie range. This represented the finest men's factory-made garments in the world. Anyone with genuine Ackerman connections was welcome, even in peacetime, in any tailoring concern in Britain.

To show their confidence, the Greens offered me a contract on the spot. I told them no, thanks. I had no great faith in contracts, which only existed to be broken. The basis of our relationship, I maintained, should be one of mutual satisfaction. We finally agreed on monthly payments, with four weeks' notice on either side to terminate the employment.

My real objection to a contract was that I feared it might complicate matters when I decided the time was ripe to pull out and join the army. But the Greens, stressing that making uniforms was vital war work and that I would therefore be in a reserved occupation and not liable to call-up, made me even more determined not to get tied down in Civvy Street. I was still straining at the leash. Nothing was going to stop me getting into this anti-Hitler war, once Bessie and the boy were reasonably well settled.

I managed to rent a little house in Bishop Auckland and moved my wife and child there from Aylesbury. Then, I applied myself to the job and, with my intimate knowledge of the trade, managed to break down and relocate the work load and so organised the production lines that the sections practically ran themselves. I got the girls substantial pay rises and, as the Green's War Office contract was on a cost plus ten per cent basis, everybody was happy.

Except me. I was still a card-carrying Communist although I didn't start any agitation in Bishop Auckland and I was at odds with the Party line anyway, because of my support for the war. A couple of nights a week I devoted to the Home Guard and every time I donned khaki, the nearest I could get to the real army, I couldn't help feeling guilty and becoming increasingly restless.

The London blitz resolved my problem. Bessie's father and mother were bombed out in the East End and came to Bishop Auckland to share our house. Bessie was overjoyed to have her folks live with her and her father quickly got some regular work with a local building firm.

This was my opportunity. Without telling Bess, I went down to the recruiting station at Darlington, had a quick medical, and signed on for the duration. I told the Greens I'd had my call-up papers and, despite their protestations about my indispensability and assurances that they would lodge an immediate appeal, insisted on my giving them the statutory month's notice.

As far as Bessie was aware, I'd been fired from the Greens for various unspecified reasons and, as I was no longer in a reserved occupation, she wasn't surprised when I received my call-up papers. I was, because, together with a four-shilling postal order and a travel warrant, I was directed to present myself at the Pioneer Corps Training Centre at Bradford. Apparently, I'd been medically graded B3 because of an eye defect. At that stage of the war, they were still pretty choosey and accepted only AI and AII men for the infantry. I'd been turned down some years ago when I applied for a rail job on the New York underground because of this sight weakness, but I'd got so used to my one good eye comfortably doing the work of two, it shook me to find that a minor disability made me less than adequate as a potential fighting man. I suppose it was my pride that received the biggest jolt, but I was in the Army now, even if it was only the Pioneers, and I determined to make the best of it and see what happened.

Chapter 16

We were billeted at Oswell Bank Junior School and started immediately on eight weeks' basic training. For me, it was a doddle. I was mustard keen and, in any event, I'd learned how to handle and fire a rifle and strip a Bren gun in the Home Guard. I dressed smartly and kept myself trim at all times, never sparing the spit and polish, even for fatigues. I determined to prove to myself and others that I was 'The Good Soldier Sam', the very antithesis of that first world war Czech, 'The Good Soldier Švejk' in the unfinished novel by Jaroslav Hasek.

I thought nobody would notice me and ask what that smart soldier was doing in the lowly Pioneers, basically the labourers and odd job utility men. However, someone up there did notice me and, whereas most of my mates were shipped from Bradford out on various attachments, I stayed on and was posted to a very cushy number in the depot itself. My job was to sort out and maintain the clothing for kitting out the new intakes. For once, according to them, the Army had fitted a round peg into a round hole. They'd figured that, as I was a tailor, I would be the ideal man for the clothing stores. How right they were was shown when I kitted out an entire new intake after only my second day on duty. The Major in charge of the Company, the Royal Engineers officer, came down in person to congratulate me.

"You know, Berkovitz," he said, "this is my first intake to look reasonably well-dressed on parade. It's obviously thanks to your expertise. I'm very pleased with you, Berkovitz. We are going to keep you. I hope you're happy here," he added as an afterthought.

"As a matter of fact, Sir," I said, "I'm not. Quite the reverse. I didn't join the Army to become a tailor. I was a tailor already. I gave it up to become a soldier."

"I'm very pleased to hear it," he told me. "But frankly, I don't know what you can do about it. I've been trying ever since the war started to get into a line regiment, but as you see, I'm still stuck here."

He must have noticed the look of utter dejection on my face, because he added quickly, "Maybe you'll be luckier than me, Berkovitz – I'll arrange for you to see the Commandant."

The following week I polished my buttons till they flashed like little mirrors when I moved, put on my best uniform, and went to the local Headquarters at Bradford to be interviewed. The Colonel in command was a real old shellback, with medal ribbons going back to the Ashanti wars, I shouldn't be surprised. He resembled Low's Colonel Blimp, but there was nothing blimpish about him. His pale blue eyes were alive with intelligence and it was clear it would take a pretty sharp character to bamboozle him.

"What's the trouble, Berkovitz?" he asked briskly. "Get it off your chest."

"Well Sir," I said. "I am hale and hearty. I'm not much over thirty. In the prime of life, you might say."

"Go on," prompted the Colonel.

"When I joined the Army, I expected a more positive role than the one I've got."

"Which is?" he said, as if he didn't know.

"Serving clothing in the stores."

The Colonel smiled and, misquoting Milton said "he also waits who stands and serves – don't you think it's a cushy enough number?"

"Too cushy," I said. "Half the British Army would give their rifles and packs to get this job; but I'm the one that's got it, and I certainly don't want it."

The Colonel was delighted. He rubbed his hands together with immense satisfaction. "Very good," he chortled. "Very good indeed. That's what I like to hear. A soldier, eh? Well, if you want to soldier I'll help you."

He glanced at my papers. "You say you're hale and hearty, but I see here you're B3. Why?"

"I think it's my eyes, Sir," I said.

"What's wrong with your eyes?" he asked.

"Nothing Sir," I assured him. "My left eye's a bit weak, that's all. In basic training I was the best shot in our platoon."

The Colonel grinned. "Left eye, you said? That's the one you close anyway. All right, leave it to me."

He reached over for the telephone and dialled a number. "Stewart," I heard him say. "I'm sending a man over. Private Berkovitz SI309 1795. I want you to do whatever you can for him." He hung up the 'phone, rose from his chair, shook my hand, and wished me luck. "On your way, soldier," were his parting words. "Things will start moving now."

When I eventually got to see Dr Stewart, he was poring over my file with a puzzled look on his face. He motioned me to sit down, concluded his inspection of the documents, slid them neatly back in the cover and leaning his elbows on the table, looked at me.

"Well, Private Berkovitz," he said. "I don't know what to do about you. I can guess what the old man wants but, according to your medical reports, there's nothing much wrong with you except for your eyes. So, I can't see, if you'll pardon the expression, how I can get you out."

"Just a minute, Sir," I said. "There's some mistake. I don't want to get out. I want to get in." From his quizzical glance I guessed he might be thinking this was some psychologically inspired ploy on my part. Only a lunatic would want to stay in the army when he had a chance of working his ticket. I hastily disabused him of the notion and went into my whole spiel all over again.

Finally, Dr Stewart nodded. "All right. Take off your jacket and let's have a look at you." He prodded perfunctorily at my chest with his stethoscope to see, I suppose, if I was still breathing, and then shone a thin concentrated beam of light onto my pupils. He spotted the bad eye immediately and checked it once again. Shaking his head, he made me look through a piece of cardboard which had a pinhole in the centre. "Private Berkovitz," he announced, "You've got a very bad eye there. Take care of the other because when that begins to deteriorate you'll be a blind man."

"I'll do that Sir," I said. "Meantime, I'll be glad if you can upgrade me." "All right," He said. "A2".

"No Sir. A1, please. Otherwise it's back to the stores for the duration."

"Very well, if you want it that way, I'll upgrade you to A1. But I'm giving you a chit for two pairs of glasses to absolve me of all responsibility and cover me in case you ever get court-martialled for firing the wrong way."

After reporting at the Company office, I left for my billet with the jaunty arm swing of an A1 infantryman. Then I sat down and dashed off a letter to a Major General, no less: Major General WDS Brownrigg, Honorary Colonel of the Sherwood Foresters. A bit of a cheek, no doubt, but the letter got to him, and probably my semi-literate scrawl now reposes as a curiosity in the Regimental archives. To explain why I wrote to General Brownrigg, among the unrelated items of useless military information plucked from the Whitechapel reference library and stuffed into my ragbag mind was a piece about the Lancashire Fusiliers winning six VCs at Gallipoli before breakfast, and another item lauding the Sherwood Foresters as the first regiment of the line after the Guards and standing on the left of them in the order of battle.

I knew I couldn't make the Guards, so it was a choice between the Fusiliers and the Foresters, nothing but the best for Berkovitz. I chose the Foresters because only the previous day there had been a paragraph in the newspaper about their distinguished Honorary Colonel, Major General Brownrigg.

At the weekend I was suddenly posted to an RAOC ammunition depot up in Scotland, at Armed Priory in the Trossachs. The Ordnance were in charge there; we, the Pioneers, as usual, supplied the muscle. We lived in Nissen huts on a big estate at Portman's Heath. We worked very hard stacking ammunition into bays, each pair of us learning to manhandle 9.2 shells weighing 360 pounds and, after a while, tossing them around as if they were half-hundredweight sacks of coal. I got so physically exhausted at night that I used to fall asleep over supper in the hut, but I could feel the effort toughening me up and it certainly did my morale the world of good.

Some three or four weeks later, I was called first thing in the morning and told to report to the Major in Charge, like my previous CO a Royal Engineers Officer.

"How the hell did you do it?" were his first words to me.

"Do what, Sir?" I asked innocently.

"Don't play games, Berkovitz," said the Major. "You know very well. I have here an order of transfer from the Pioneers to the Sherwood Foresters. I've been waiting forever to get into an infantry battalion. How in bloody hell did you do it?"

Once more I aired my odyssey, by now a word-perfect set piece complete with dramatic pauses for effect. "And I feel if I'm not in the infantry," I added as a coda, "I'm not really soldiering. I'm wearing ammunition boots but I'm not a real foot soldier. I'm violently opposed to Hitler and having been so vocal about it for so long, I felt it was time I put my guts where my mouth was. I've no illusions about war. I don't think lumps of hot metal will be of much benefit to my health. But it's my firm conviction that I've got to be upfront with the infantry where the shit's flying, and that's it."

"Very commendable," said the Major drily. "But it doesn't answer my question. I've written letters too, and look where it's got me. Nowhere."

Chapter 17

I was supposed to leave the following day and make my way to Caister Camp near Yarmouth, but the Major, a very decent chap, had discovered from my papers that my family lived in Bishop Auckland, and offered to let me off right away so I could have a few hours at home. He suggested I went via Edinburgh, and calling the office orderly to make out the movement orders, the CO sped me on my way and wished me luck.

I was so excited by this stroke of good fortune that I left my kit bag in the canvas-top utility van that ran me to Edinburgh and my respirator and other webbing equipment somewhere on the train. My wife was overjoyed at my unexpected arrival, likewise my son, now sitting up and taking notice and howling like a distraught coyote whenever I left his side. It was hell's own job for Bess to distract his attention when I had to leave the following morning and I slipped through the kitchen into the garden and out the back way before Barry could give tongue and wake up all the neighbours.

I arrived at the Foresters' depot in Caister that night around twelve o'clock and walked into the Guard Room carrying only my rifle.

"Who are you?" asked the corporal on duty gruffly. "Whoever you are, you're late." He stuck out his hand. "Where are your papers?"

"Haven't got 'em," I said. "In the rush to get down here I left them in Scotland."

"Where's your kit? Where's your gasmask?"

I tried to explain: "I left that here…forgot this there…"

The corporal looked at me with mounting incredulity when I ran out of what he assumed were simply poor excuses, and rebuked me more in sorrow than in anger.

"You'd better check that your fly buttons are done up in case you've lost anything else."

I was sure I was heading for the glasshouse but, strangely enough, that mild reprimand was the worst that happened to me. I slept overnight on a camp bed in the Guard Room and in the morning reported for duty with B Company the First Battalion Sherwood Foresters. I expect showing up with only a rifle didn't overly arouse the curiosity of these tough young regulars. Veterans of Dunkirk, some of them had been glad to come back to Britain simply with whole skins. I probably struck them as just a stupid old goof and the plain fact of the matter was that, at thirty-six, I was coming up for twice their average age.

They'd been pretty badly mauled by Hitler's Stukas on the roads and on the beaches escaping from France, and the regiment was now being made up to strength. I fitted into my section without much trouble, though they detached a sergeant to train me on my own for a few days so that I could catch up with the specifics of Foresters' drill routine. Being an able-bodied and reasonably intelligent person, and consumed by a desire to do well so that no-one could question my fitness to sustain the rigours of front-line combat, there were no problems. I passed with ease tests on the Bren gun, rifle, and grenade and took assault courses, route marches – eighteen miles in five hours with rifle and full pack – and night recce schemes, in my stride.

The weeks dragged on. Nobody seemed in a particular hurry to get back into the war, apart from Private Berkovitz, who hadn't been in it yet. Then, one day the word went around that a draft of fifteen men was required for overseas service with the 13th Battalion. I made all speed towards the Company office, asked to see the Regimental Sergeant Major and immediately volunteered.

"Stand easy, Private Berkovitz," said the Regimental Sergeant Major (RSM) gazing with approval at my ramrod posture. "Now, why are you in such a hurry to leave us? I've been keeping my eye on you. You're a smart soldier. I could always use a good man on my permanent staff."

Here it came again! Everyone with authority in the Army tried to put me off or get me out but, the more obstacles that were placed in my path, the more determined I was to surmount them and dive into the fray. As I didn't answer immediately – my regular spiel wasn't quite right in this context – the RSM obviously thought I was playing shy and might need a little more coaxing. "Well, Berkovitz?" he urged, "Stay. You'll have a chance to grow here."

"All I'll grow here, Sir, I said, is old. With respect, Sargeant Major, I'm old enough already. Too old. I'm thirty-six. Time's not on my side. I don't know what's in store for me, but there's no point in hanging about now. I want to be where the action is."

He wished me all the best and I went off home on six days' leave with instructions to proceed afterwards to the 13th Sherwood Foresters Holding Battalion at their Colchester Camp, where I would be part of the Reserve Company. There, we were confined to town, all leave cancelled. For five weeks we marched and countermarched while the mobilisation stores built up, until we were suddenly given six days' embarkation leave and told it was to be the last. No lenient treatment from now on. Anyone not getting back on the dot would be AWOL and liable for the severest wartime penalties.

At the end of six wonderful days at home came what I hated and feared most, because I was always at my most vulnerable: the goodbyes. I adored my wife and worshipped my son and hated having to go without knowing whether I would see them again. But I refused to allow anything to dent my resolution – fast becoming an obsession – to get into the thick of the battle. So, I slunk away from Bishop Auckland in the early hours while my son was still asleep, with a goodbye kiss on his forehead and a final tearful embrace from Bess.

After my embarkation leave, things at Colchester tightened up. We were allowed into the town but had to be back in camp by 10.30 pm. There were no late passes for anybody. One morning I was called in to the Company office to see my CO, Captain Macpherson, a sturdy little Scot who had worked his way up from the ranks.

What now? I wondered. Were they going to turf me out of this combat unit at the last moment? But my luck still held.

"Berkovitz," the CO said, "Will you take a stripe?"

"Yes, Sir" I answered with alacrity. "I will. It'll be an honour."

"I'm glad," said Macpherson. "Your platoon Corporal recommended you. Tomorrow there will be a Special – when we give orders. Come here at 5.30 pm in your best uniform. You'll meet the adjutant and be made up to Lance Corporal."

As was my wont when I had any big news to impart, I wrote to Bess right away: 'When you next send me a letter', I told her, 'I want you to address me as Lance Corporal Samuel Berkovitz. I've got my foot firmly on the bottom rung of the ladder. I'm now a Lance Corporal. Twenty-two more promotions and I'll be a Field Marshal.'

At 4.30 pm next day, I had my best uniform on an hour early, but I was afraid to sit down in case I spoiled the crease in my trousers. At 5 pm, the bugle sounded three Gs. It meant rush on the double. There was no parade. Warrant Officers, NCOs, all hurried across to headquarters. When they came out, all leave was cancelled, all passes were cancelled and everyone confined to barracks. We were moving in the morning. My excitement at seeing some real action at last was slightly tinged with disappointment. I had suffered the quickest demotion in the history of the British Army. As it had never appeared on Orders, I'd lost my Lance Corporal's stripe before I got it.

Chapter 18

Once again Private Berkovitz, S., I entrained with the rest of the 13th Battalion and boarded the 'Britannic' at Greenock on May 29th, 1942. A big, comfortable ship of some 27,000 tons, it was carrying around 8,000 soldiers to whichever theatre of operations had indented for our services. It took two days to complete the loading and on May 31st, in company with about twenty other ships, we sailed down the Clyde into the open Channel. From there we moved into the Irish Sea where we teamed up with sixteen more ships and picked up another dozen or so off Northern Ireland, making the convoy up to around forty-eight vessels.

Majestically, we ploughed a wide arc through the North Atlantic, then gradually moved South. Our naval escort comprised a big sixteen-inch gun ship, the 'Nelson', steaming in the centre for heavy protection with a complementary cruiser attached. Three busy destroyers on anti-submarine patrol also raced around, whooping alongside the slower vessels like sheepdogs chivvying tardy lambs into the fold. In addition, there was a big merchantman converted into an auxiliary carrier, with a dozen light planes on board for scouting.

We slept in hammocks below decks. The rest of our lives on board revolved around the mess decks, where each section had its own dining area and meals were served at long tables. I don't remember much about the food – after all, this was more than forty years ago – except that I slung most of mine through the porthole. That didn't worry me as long as there was plenty of tea – a penny a cup, and wads – a penny per cake – and the occasional decent bit of grub bought, or liberated, from the cook's galley.

As we moved South it got warmer and we took to sleeping out in the open air on blankets laid on the floor of the decks. This was the life of Riley, almost an extended holiday cruise. Here were no special military activities apart from an odd guard, a weekly parade for checking weapons, and the regular physical training exercises. There were a couple of lectures we had to attend, but they were of a general nature, mainly concerned with hygiene in hot climates, and didn't give us a clue as to exactly where we were heading. One of the lads claimed he saw bales of tropical gear hoisted aboard the Britannic with the stores and this at least gave a sense of direction to some of the other wild rumours floating about, though we still had no idea where we were destined for, the Middle East, the Far East, Africa or possibly Australia. Some of the cynical old sweats said the bales had probably been shipped on board to confuse the enemy and we'd all end up in Iceland.

At Freetown, we took on further supplies and fresh water and then heard there'd be a stopover, with a spell on shore either at Cape Town or Durban. We'd been afloat for about a month and were looking forward eagerly to a few days on dry land. So far it had been an utterly uneventful voyage, not a plane, an enemy submarine or surface vessel encountered anywhere. Not a single untoward incident. It all seemed too good to last; and it didn't.

One morning, just before we arrived at Durban, the ship's tannoy sounded the alarm with 'Attention! Attention! All personnel assemble at Company Stations.' We paraded on deck at once and Captain Macpherson, accompanied by two young lieutenants and our Company Sergeant Major, stepped in front of us. As we stood to attention, Macpherson held a signal in his hand but had no need to refer to it. He knew the contents by heart.

"I have some very sad news, men," he said. "Tobruk has fallen."

A gasp of dismay shook the ranks. From all over the ship came similar explosions of disbelief as each company was briefed by its officers. The decks vibrated like a cauldron on the boil. Then followed a shocked silence. Singapore surrendering not so many weeks before, we could understand. The guns were pointing the wrong way. But impregnable Tobruk, that heavily defended fortress, how could that fall?

"Despite this reverse, men," Macpherson spoke on, not a tremor in his beautifully pronounced Scottish vowels, "we carry on soldiering, quietly confident till we win."

He marched off with the officers and we were dismissed. The parade dissolved into restless little knots as we recovered our tongues.

"I suppose that's where we'll be going – the Middle East," said Farnwell, one of my mates.

"Too late," grumbled another.

"Don't see why," broke in Cooney, a greying veteran, one of the real old sweats. "We should get there just in time to be captured. With a present of all our brand-new equipment. Just like in Singapore."

But it was this same Cooney who, lying near me on his blanket that night, his hands clasped behind his head, after a quiet smoke below decks and a jaundiced review of the day's events, summed it up as he saw the situation.

"You know what, Berko," he said. "At the end of the day we'll still do the buggers in."

Later, I found most of my comrades on board felt the same as Cooney. Though they didn't put it in so many words, they felt that, despite yet another military disaster, despite inept politicians and incompetent generals in the field, the British soldier would muddle through to victory the way he always did. And I must say I was much comforted.

A few days before we were due to dock, we were informed officially that India was to be our final destination. Actually, we didn't have to be told; we knew already. A week or so earlier, well out into the Indian Ocean, we were able to get a fix on the sun. By placing matches on the deck, we found the angle the sun made pointed East-North-East, and that could only mean India.

Every day thereafter we anxiously scanned the horizon for a sight of land. Cooney, who had served in India as a boy soldier, mocked our excitement. "Don't worry," he jeered. "You won't miss India. You'll be able to smell her before you see her. You'll know you're there, even miles out to sea, by the stink. It's the odour of open drains and elephant shit and 600 million sweating bodies."

I don't know whether Cooney's words triggered off my imagination, but I could have sworn I could smell something putrid in the air about the time we sighted Bombay.

It was August 1st when we arrived. We spent three days in dock waiting for the trains to be assembled and the stores unloaded from the ship. I was, as usual, pretty broke. Most of my pay had vanished on board in games of Bingo, Brag and Crown and Anchor, and most of what was left had disappeared down my gullet in endless relays of char and wads. I borrowed a couple of chips – two rupees – worth about 18 old pence each, from the Corporal who ran our Bingo school and, in the afternoon, went ashore in search of something to eat.

I found it at the Indian Women's Services Club on the recreational area, known as the Maidan. For four annas – fivepence – I got a colossal meal of mashed potatoes, fried eggs, sausages, bacon and as much tea made with real milk and sugar as I could swallow. Next day I was there lunchtime and evening for the same again.

On the third day, we were all told to go ashore but get back on station before midnight, ready to move off in the morning. I bloated myself with two big meals, in between mooching around the bazaars, my feeling of wellbeing extending even to giving away a couple of annas in baksheesh. By evening, replete, I still had five annas left. Ambling along in front of me I recognised the lanky figure of Tommy Dodd. Like me a cockney and, like me also, perpetually hungry, I wasn't very pally with him at that time as he was in a different Company. Much younger than me, he'd falsified his age to join the Territorials in July 1939 and was drafted into the regular Army in August after only three weeks' training. Now, age 17, he'd already had two and a half years' service under his belt. We had, apart from the metropolitan connection, something else in common. Tommy was also a *spieler*. He would gamble on anything. He'd put his money down on which mosquito would bite you first.

"How's it going, Tommy?" I said when I caught up with him.

"Lousy!" he grunted.

"What's up?" I asked.

"I'm skint," he said.

"Who ain't? You, me and the whole British Army," I replied

"Sam," Tommy said morosely. "I'm bloody well starving. I've been here days in Bombay and I haven't had a proper meal."

"Well, you can start singing Good King Wenceslas." I said. "Christmas is here. I can direct you to the best canteen in the world. The sort of place you only dream about. The soldiers in Valhalla haven't got a canteen like this. Take the first turning on the right, where the Maidan is and a few doors down, there's the entrance to paradise, the Indian Women's Services Club."

Tommy's expression became even more gloomy. "And what do I do for money?" he asked. "I told you. This is the Feast of Stephen." I told him as I gave him my last five annas and waved away his feeble protests.

"For this," I assured him, "I guarantee you can get as much as you can eat. And more."

He had a tremendous nosh-up and when I met him later at the station he was puffing away happily at an English cigarette from a packet of Woodbines he'd also bought at the canteen.

"Sam," he sighed contentedly, "You saved my life. I'll never forget you for this."

I didn't regard it as any particular big deal. I knew Tommy or any of the boys would, in similar circumstances, do the same for me and I quite forgot about it. But Doddy didn't forget. Almost three years later, when I was stationed in Lucknow, the postman came in shouting "Corporal Berkovitz, Sahib, Corporal Berkovitz, Sahib."

"It sounds like my name," I said. "What do you want?" He gave me a letter and showed me a money order for twenty rupees that had already been cashed. Both were from Tommy Dodd. He'd had a lucky turn at the horses and remembered me. I gave the postman one rupee, which pleased him mightily, and ate like a horse for two weeks till the other nineteen were exhausted.

Next morning, August 4th, we boarded a very long train, which began to chug up towards the Punjab. The carriages were spacious, not particularly clean, but reasonably comfortable, and the train was above all functional: it started and stopped as required and got you there, wherever 'there' was. Over the previous century, the much-maligned British had unified India by covering the huge sub-continent with a network of canals and efficient railways. We were probably the best thing to happen to India since the Mogul Emperors.

We had two meals a day on the train, breakfast and an evening meal, mostly corned beef and biscuits, and finally arrived at Rawalpindi, where we were to undergo a period of acclimatisation.

Three months later, we were on the move again, this time to Secunderabad in the Deccan, a large plain jutting into the Indian Ocean. It was considered to be a likely invasion point for the Japanese because of the flat open country. No sooner had we settled in Secunderabad's Wheeler Lines, more a throwback to pre-war Cavalry barracks nomenclature than rumours of a big flap were in the air. This was fuelled by the information that we were being converted immediately into an armoured regiment. A couple of General Lee tanks arrived on one of the squares and we were all issued with bush hats. There was a sudden burst of activity with crash courses in just about everything.

Now Trouper Berkovitz, I spent six intensive weeks learning to be a signaller. It was dah-dah-didah most of the time, with lamps and semaphore intervening. I got so immersed in dah-dah-di-dah, I automatically began to read messages from woodpeckers hammering at trees. We were also introduced to the latest wireless sets, which had quite a good range, and we went out on all sorts of situations to make sure we knew how to operate them correctly.

I thoroughly enjoyed all this activity and welcomed it as widening my military horizons. It made me realise that the modern British soldier is a compendium of skilled trades. Not only does he march and shoot, but he's a driver, a bit of a mechanic, a bit of an engineer, an electrician, a navigator, a muleteer, a wireless operator and an explosives expert as well.

Towards the end of my wireless training course I was summoned to the Colonel's office. I knew I'd done exceptionally well and was expecting a reward. I got it. I was fired. They chucked me off the course and, indeed, out of the armoured regiment altogether. I became Private Berkovitz again. The Adjutant had come across an Army Council Instruction (ACI), which laid down that the son of an enemy alien could not be allowed access to a wireless set in the field. I had forgotten that, because my father was Rumanian, I was technically in that category as Rumania had joined the Axis powers in 1940. Of course, I was bitterly disappointed, but neither I nor the Colonel could buck an ACI. However, he was very nice about it and pointed out that, in the turnover into an armoured regiment, we were now a couple of hundred men above establishment anyway and, owing to my age, I was bound to be one of the soldiers surplus to requirements who had to be re-assigned elsewhere.

I was very upset, but perked up a little when I discovered that Tommy Dodd – the Colonel obviously considered him to be too young just as I was too old – was among the two hundred rejects, along with a few more of my old mates. A couple of days later, we said goodbye to everyone and, temporarily unattached, entrained at Secunderabad for Deolali transit camp. Due to its unpleasant environment and the boredom associated with it, there was a conception of it in the army so strong it filtered through into the language of civvy street. A soldier would tap his forehead with the tips of his fingers and say of a comrade 'he's gone doolally' meaning 'he's lost his mind' or 'gone bonkers'.

Deolali was an enormous staging camp where troops came from all over India to be re-graded, retrained and re-deployed. The huge cantonment also housed a medical centre with its average quota of doctors, psychologists and the usual number of generally mentally sick and the odd, opportunist skrimshankers. But the hospital represented only a small proportion of the Camp's facilities. It had everything. There were even, I heard, a couple of officially-tolerated brothels within the lines or close by. My comrades, lusty virile young men, took full advantage of these delights. They tried several times to get me to come along with them, but I always declined. They didn't understand and I couldn't be bothered to tell them that I was committed to conserving all my energies simply to stay abreast of them at every level. Without conscious effort, they maintained high standards of mental alertness and physical fitness, whereas I knew if I was not up to scratch in a battle, sluggish reflexes could cost me my life. I had to be a good soldier. More than good, I had to be the best.

I'd always laughed at Party zealots like Nat Cohen, with messianic fires burning in their eyes. Yet here was I acting the same way, like some eager young acolyte in the Temple of Mars. I lived and thought only soldiering. I tired myself out and slept like a log and, when I dreamed, I dreamt sometimes of Bess, but more often of food and clearing out enemy strongpoints singlehanded.

Chapter 19

After two weeks at Deolali, movement orders went up – a hundred of us were detailed to join the Lancashire Fusiliers stationed at Cawnpore (modern Kapur), in Uttar Pradesh, the site of a massacre of British soldiers and civilians during the Indian rebellion of 1857. I was delighted to become one of this crack regiment, even more so when I learned that Tommy Dodd and a couple more of my mates would be coming along with me. Next morning, we marched down to the station and a day and a half later we paraded before the Fusiliers' RSM.

We were incorporated into different companies and started on routine drills, guards, marches and an occasional canal crossing. This went on for four or five weeks and I finally managed to get in a long-awaited 28 days' leave. I went to Bombay where I haunted the bazaars for bargains, sending home packets of tea and silk scarves for Bess and coloured little native gewgaws for the boy. My meals came cheap, courtesy of the Indian Women's Services Club in the Maidan. I also paid a couple of visits to the Lakshmi Race Track. Lakshmi is the Goddess of Luck but I never did get on well with women and, true to form, Lakshmi didn't smile on me at all.

When I got back to Cawnpore, broke but happy, I found a scarcely suppressed air of excitement about the camp. We were expecting a visit in the afternoon from a military big-wig, someone really special they said, and we were detailed to parade at 4.30 pm. It didn't excite me overmuch. I'd had these upper echelon brass hats before. They'd give us another pep talk and disappear. Well, I didn't need any more pep talks. I wanted action. Maybe this time it was for real. Maybe we'd be shipped out to the Arakan in Burma, the only sector where the Japanese were operating in strength and where, to tell the truth, we were getting one hell of a bashing because somehow we couldn't adapt to the terrain.

Our visitor, at first glance, hardly looked like someone in the Churchill mould. Of medium height and wiry build, to judge from where I stood in the square, he wore drill trousers and a loose bush jacket topped by a khaki pith helmet above a lean, bearded face pierced by two sharp eyes and fringed by a growth of dark beard. He didn't speak right away. He motioned us to close in a bit and then looked at us, rank by rank, as if he wanted to memorise our faces. Using the oldest of actors' tricks, he waited till he grabbed our full attention before he uttered a single word.

"My name is Orde Wingate," he began. His voice wasn't loud but his words were clearly enunciated and audible to everyone on the parade ground. "I am here to tell you, men, that I've developed some new tactics. They come under the heading of Long-Range Penetration. I am organising some new groups for that purpose and this battalion of the Lancashire Fusiliers has been selected to form one of these self-contained groups, or columns, together with the King's Liverpool, the Cameronians, and a Gurkha battalion and assorted service units. You will become part of a Special Force comprising four brigades as a complete division, plus a fifth brigade which is already formed and functioning, plus service troops, plus a special air command that will be manned by the RAF and our American friends, but which will be seconded to us and entirely at our disposal. As I said, the tactics will be new, hence your activity training will be entirely different from that to which you have been accustomed. It's going to be tough. Very tough. It's going to make you sweat, but sweat saves blood. The more you sweat, the more blood you'll save. When you're tired, and you will be, I promise you, very tired, that's when you're most vulnerable. I'll teach you to be on your guard. Always. Every minute. Every second. I'll teach you to move in the jungle. To live in the jungle like a native. You'll be supplied from the air. You'll never have to look back to see what's happening behind you because it doesn't matter what's happening behind you. We won't wait for things to happen. We'll impose our will on what's to take place. Don't worry about food or ammunition. What supplies we don't take in on our backs will be dropped from the skies. It's perfectly feasible. We've already tried it with one brigade and I assure you it works. Now, if you're imagining you won't be able to cope with the demands of Special Force, forget it. You can. I am convinced that any British Infantry Battalion, properly trained, will respond to any reasonable demands such as I have outlined. You men particularly, as Northerners, should have no problems. I like the mixture of artisans and agricultural workers in North Country battalions. It's a fine combination and here, in the

Lancashire Fusiliers, I'm sure I have the very best. So, let us to our tasks. I know the Lord will lead us through the wilderness and guide our arms to smite the Amalekites!"

He stopped, nodded as if to imply that was all we needed to know, gave a sort of half salute, and walked off. The spell was broken and the square became talkative, individual soldiers again. It was one of the unforgettable moments of my Army life, like hearing the announcement aboard the Britannic that Tobruk had fallen. There, however, with Macpherson's tragic news, our morale slipped momentarily into the deepest slough of despondency. Here, Wingate's words lifted up our hearts. Even the irrepressible Cooney was favourably impressed. "Looks like this bloke knows what he's talking about," he conceded.

At that time, I'd never heard of Wingate and had no idea of his distinguished military provenance in Ethiopia and his reputation as a tactician with the Haganah in Palestine. But, starting from scratch on that sweltering Cawnpore parade ground, his personality was overwhelming. He struck me as a man with a viable vision despite the odd, little bible-punching homily at the end. Probably he fancied himself deep down as an Old Testament prophet.

I never saw Wingate again. In March of the following year, at the peak of Chindit activities, he was killed in an air crash. Two newspapermen he had brought along in the plane for on-the-spot briefing also died.

With Wingate gone, the drive went out of what remained of the Chindit Campaign. Colonel Lentaine, a former Gurkha Officer with a fine record, took over Command, though most of us thought Major Mike Calvert, a tough regular, who had been close to Wingate from the start, and had already led a Chindit column, should have had the job. But no-one could take Wingate's place, anyway. He was Churchill's white-haired boy and, we heard, could get straight through to him at any time. Wingate's daring military ideas had always appealed to the old buccaneer. Churchill had himself suffered when his own unorthodox strategy had, as in Gallipoli, been frustrated by the hidebound military establishment in the field. Now, the same breed of General, like the crusty American, 'Vinegar Joe' Stillwell, operating with a Chinese division on our flanks, who never had too much liking for Wingate's antics anyhow, thought we had carried on our independent existence long enough and wound up the whole operation: he re-absorbed the Chindits into the Army proper. Wingate's death, however, was still some nine months ahead when we moved from Cawnpore to Orcher in June 1943.

Orcher was sited on the holy River Yamuna or Jumna. It was in full spate when we got there, with a current flowing so fast and wild that we had to sling a cable across it and work our way clinging to it hand over fist to reach the opposite bank. After a couple of weeks, the rains subsided and it was possible to swim across without help from the cable or fear of being swept away.

We newly-fledged Chindits (the name came from our divisional flash, the dog-faced lion guardian of the temple) began training afresh there, this time specifically for jungle warfare as laid down in Wingate's Long-Range Penetration manual.

"In two weeks I'll teach you all there is to know about mules," said our instructor, Major Mike Calvert. Thus spoke the voice of jungle training. Calvert was that resolute, resourceful soldier who knew more about jungle warfare than any other man in India. "Now you can get a mule to water, but you can't force him to cross. However, once he gets to know and trust you, then he'll follow you anywhere. Like this." Suiting the action to his words, Calvert grabbed the bridle of his mule and marched him straight into the swollen Jumna until only the top of the animal's head was visible.

They swam together in a short circle and then, leading the animal ashore, he resumed his lesson. Calvert explained the reason for the mule's obstinacy in not getting into the water whenever we ourselves had previously tried to coax them in. "A mule is even lower in the water than a horse," he told us. 'With his neck stretched out, only his nostrils, his eyes and his ears are visible, so any patch of water looks like an ocean to him. But lead him in confidently and talk to him, and you'll have no further problems."

For the next two weeks, I shared my life with Pancho, my mule, and we became good friends. I coaxed him into the river Jumna every day the Calvert way and he loved it. If I packed even a little too much weight on one side, he would look at me reproachfully until I adjusted the balance. He was intelligent, hardy, and very reliable and perfectly capable of living off the country when there was no fodder.

I was quite upset when, at the end of the two weeks, I had to return Pancho to his muleteer. 'Goodbye, old son', I whispered in his ear. He looked at me with his big yellow-flecked eyes but, although I'm sure he understood, he remained mute, his vocal chords having been cut so that his baying wouldn't disturb the silence of our clandestine operations behind the enemy lines.

We started regular marches through the jungle, rehearsed river crossings with assault boats and learned how to clamber on and off gliders, always adapting our daily exercises to cope with the difficulties of the varied terrain. Our Gurkhas showed us how to make use of the ubiquitous clumps of bamboo proliferating in the jungle. By splitting the thin trunks and shaving them off, we made lengths of string that had the tensile strength of wire. We could wrap up all our gear in groundsheets, tie the bundles with strips of bamboo and float them across a river without the contents getting soaked. We also learned that, at a pinch, you could get water from the female bamboo, the only visible difference from the male being that the female was thicker.

By late November, with our rigorous training schedule nearing completion, I was attached to the HQ 'Specialist' Company and, one Sunday, we set off on yet another endurance march, this time only three days – a piece of cake. I was looking forward to it – our final ground exercise – as the heat had somewhat abated, and three days march I thought I could do on one leg.

Corporal Blackwell was in charge of my HQ Section, with a Lance Corporal named Davis. I was next in line, number two, on the Bren Gun, with seven others behind me. Blackwell – always Blackie to the men – was a fine, strapping NCO who'd already done seven years in India and was due to go home. He'd postponed his return because he was eager to go in with the Chindits.

When we started off, all chirpy and smiling, Blackwell helped me on with my kit. I always had a tendency to carry my kit a bit low and he gave me his usual little lecture, reminding me that the higher the pack, the less strain on the back. We marched for three hours, stopping for a few minutes at the end of each hour. Starting off on our fourth hour, Blackwell didn't look too good.

"What's up?" I asked him.

He shrugged his shoulders. "Feeling a bit rough. It'll pass."

I wasn't so sure. Earlier in the day he'd complained about his chronic constipation and I'd told him my trouble since landing in Bombay was exactly the opposite, a loose bowel action.

Blackwell grinned. "Maybe we ought to get together more often," he said.

My problem was sometimes uncomfortable, but not really dangerous. Cooney and other old India hands weren't too worried about mild dysentery, but had warned me to avoid becoming too constipated in malarial country. I kept an anxious eye on Blackwell just ahead of me and, as we halted for the next period, I saw him totter and crumple up on the ground. We whistled up a couple of medicos from another Company in our area and they lifted him on to a stretcher. They said they would take him to Jhanis hospital. He opened his eyes during a brief moment of consciousness, waved a languid hand at me, then blacked out again and was carried to an ambulance and whisked off to hospital.

The march continued and my first day ended without any more bother. I even had a full water bottle which, for me, represented a considerable achievement as I'd managed to control my thirst *en route* by chewing on a couple of limes. We bivouacked, cooked a meal, had a wash down and slept. Next morning, I got up fresh as a daisy, the only cloud on my horizon being some concern about what was happening to Corporal Blackwell.

I completed a full second day's march and, after supper before bedding down, sat chatting with the lads gathered round a little fire we'd started, mainly for the smoke, to keep the mosquitos off. The flies were a menace. You only had to cut your finger in the bush and, if you left it uncovered for more than a few seconds, a cluster of nasty little green flies would be buzzing around infecting it. Together with the mosquitos, the flies probably killed more British soldiers than the Japanese, even on garrison duties. In the jungle, we used to protect ourselves against mosquitos on sentry duty by wearing gloves and yashmaks at night, and we couldn't sleep without an insect repellent cream covering face and hands.

On the third day I started off in the pink, feeling I could go on this way for ever. We stopped in the afternoon for a drink and a bully beef sandwich. Then I suddenly began to feel warm. I had a sort of choking feeling round my neck, as if I was wearing too-tight a collar. As the day progressed, I kept asking the time. It seemed to be passing unbearably slowly and I got hotter and hotter until I felt I would burst. I began to lurch around like a drunken sailor. One of the officers noticed my staggering gait and took in the situation at once.

"Let me have the Bren, Berkovitz." he said, "I'll carry it for a bit."

"No, Sir," I replied firmly, hanging on to the gun like grim death. "I'll manage."

He gave me a very peculiar look and moved on. I wouldn't give him the gun because I didn't want to show any sign of weakness. I knew that, at 38, I was way past the optimum age for a Chindit and was already physically suspect merely because of my years. An even more powerful reason for not giving up my Bren gun was that its weight kept me rooted to the ground. I felt that if I relinquished possession I'd float off into the treetops. The world was spinning round me and I knew I was on the point of flaking out, but I staggered on till the final hour, guided by the arm of the man behind me and, when we finally halted, everything went black and I collapsed.

The next thing I heard through clouds of cotton wool swimming round my head was a small voice from a long way off saying very clearly: "Good heavens! Look at this temperature. 105! – This man is burning up. Get him over to that stream and keep throwing water over him till the ambulance comes."

I recall being driven quickly over a bumpy road at great speed, then being moved into a building, my face gripped in a vice, strong hands forcing my mouth open and bitter quinine being poured down my throat. I was laid down flat on the bed and then my head cleared briefly as if by magic.

An orderly in a starched white coat approached.

"Where am I?" I asked him.

"Jhansi Hospital," he told me. That was where they had taken Corporal Blackwell. "Where's Blackie?" I asked. "Still here?"

"Who?"

"Blackie. He came in on Sunday."

"No-one of that name admitted. Sure, he was sent to Jhansi?"

"Sure," I said. "The medics told me. Corporal Blackwell, he came in on Sunday."

"Ah," said the orderly. "Corporal Blackwell. That's different. Corporal Blackwell did come in on Sunday. He died on Sunday morning and was buried on Sunday afternoon." In that short blaze of lucidity, I recorded the information in the same matter of fact way it was imparted and, strangely comforted, I drifted off into blessed darkness.

That's the way malaria strikes us Europeans in the tropics. No matter how big and tough you are, you can be laid low at any moment by a tiny marauding insect. In the jungle you just had to sleep under a net. Without one, the mosquitos simply wouldn't let you rest. They'd bite, but you got used to that and hardly felt it at all. What kept you awake was that the little buggers were so persistent and so noisy with it. Even covered by a net, you watched them ceaselessly moving up and down like flies, angrily probing for any little hole they could enlarge to get at you. They were after your blood. It was their way of life. You were a perambulating cafeteria, supplying drinks for mosquitos and food for flies.

I often thought that the mosquitos, the flies and the termites could, if they got together, wipe all traces of human habitation off the face of the earth. Fortunately, they were always too busy exterminating each other. The blind termites can't stand direct sunlight: they burrow under and devour everything in their path. They chew up huge trees. They creep unseen under a layer of sand, covering themselves as they progress and eat the trunk until it's a shell you can literally push over with a gentle shove. Nature, however, has its revenge, as I was lucky enough to witness in Cawnpore. Once a year the young leave the huge hillock the adult termites have thrown up, emerging from holes in the ground, male and female, to mate and make their own nests. They're equipped with wings, strong enough only for the few minutes' flight to a new location. Billions of them rise in a dense grey cloud and, in the brief period they are airborne, every bird in the vicinity swoops down to gobble them up. When the termites land and shake off their wings, every spider on the ground, every scorpion, every lizard, every snake and particularly every red and black killer ant is waiting to gorge on their soft, white bodies. Despite this annual holocaust, however, enough of them always survive to start new colonies which will, in their turn, breed billions more white ants to be decimated, except for those that rise again and multiply to be slaughtered every year *ad infinitum.*

We were never bothered overmuch by the larger predators. Tigers and other animals were rarely seen, but the leeches, which materialised at every canal and river crossing, were regarded by the boys as loathsome and somehow unclean. Actually, they were the reverse: if you applied the tip of a burning cigarette or match to them, they dropped off your skin with the sucked blood they'd taken on board. Attempting to pull them off was asking for trouble as their heads became embedded in your flesh and quickly suppurated.

My hero, Alexander the Great, is on record as using leeches to cure his wounds and, until fairly recently, they even used leeches for some delicate forms of bloodletting at the London Hospital in Whitechapel. They were supplied by a Russian chemist, Lief, who ran a pharmacy at the top of my street (Cannon Street Road) in Commercial Road. I never could quite come to terms with the insect life in India. At night you only had to strike a match for bats to materialise and huge moths would dart recklessly at the flame until they burned their wings. But they were merely a nuisance.

The pestilential, malaria-bearing mosquitos were the worst – the real killers. Creeping, burrowing, flying or crawling, the insects were all part and parcel of what I finally came to recognise as an unchangeably hostile environment for Europeans. I simply could not get used to the suddenness with which death struck. You'd speak to someone in the morning and, in the afternoon, you'd be detailed for his funeral party. Unlike my experience with Blackie, I'd detect absolutely nothing wrong with a man, then he'd be taken bad and be dead in an hour. I'd always expected a little time between a soldier suddenly falling ill, and his dying. In India, however, death came out of nowhere.

We had a respected Company Commander called 'Cushy' Kayer. I didn't see him, but one morning was told he was sick. A couple of hours later there was a firing party and a funeral detachment to bury him. Whenever you went on a march along well-used roads, you'd come across little mounds of stones by the wayside with the names of young British officers, faithful servants of the Raj, who'd died suddenly on duty thirty, forty, fifty years ago, and more.

The big trouble with malaria is that it was so hard to control. I was walking along with a mate of mine, Farnwell, on leave in Bombay. He was flush and had promised to loan me ten rupees to tide me over on the way back to Cawnpore. Suddenly, he began to shiver and collapsed at my feet. I got him into an ambulance and when he came to I reminded him about the money. "Sure," he said, and got his hand half-way in his pocket when he blacked out again. As they were taking him into the hospital he regained consciousness long enough to drag out the ten chips for me and say in a whisper, "See you, Sam."

There's no how, why or wherefore, no rhyme or reason about malaria. After my Orcher dose, I had four more bouts during the next three years of my Indian stint, one attack set off merely by a cool breeze blowing through a window. My pal, Hymie Olinsky, saw service in Egypt, Algiers and Morocco, and didn't exhibit any of the malarial symptoms till he was back home on leave in England. They treated him for two weeks, gave him another week's leave and, when he got back to his unit abroad, he collapsed again.

Returning to Orcher after fourteen days in Jhansi Hospital, my heart sank when I found the HQ Company had already left camp for the assembly area. Next morning the CO, Major Shuttleworth, sent for me.

"How're you feeling, Berkovitz?" he enquired.

"Fine Sir," I said. "Fit as a fiddle."

"Well, you don't look it," he said. "You must have copped a pretty bad dose. You still look a bit shaky to me. Take a chair if you like," he added kindly.

"No thanks." I straightened up. "I'm perfectly alright, Sir. Rarin' to go."

"Ah! That's what I wanted to talk to you about, Berkovitz. I suppose you can guess why I sent for you?"

"I reckon so." I said. You are going to tell me I'm not going in."

"Correct. You're not. I'm sending you off to Sillong for ten days in the hills to recuperate. No flies there. No mosquitos."

"Thank you, Sir." I said. "And after?"

"After," he told me, "You'll come back here to Orcher. That takes us near enough to Christmas and then the rest of the column will be on its way."

"Including me?"

"Afraid not," he said. "Our establishment is complete. We can't airlift you to your own mob now because we don't know where they are, and when you get back they could be a hundred miles further away."

"What happens to me?" I asked.

"You're being posted to the airstrip at Assam." He said. "We need some good men there."

My face dropped and he hurriedly attempted to soften the blow.

"Don't be so glum, Berkovitz. You'll still be one of us, a Chindit. They're all Chindits there, under Colonel Lord, a jolly good fellow. One of the best!"

I'd heard of Colonel Lord before. He'd been in charge of dropping supplies by air to the first Chindit column. Blokes who came out told me they'd often lifted their eyes to the skies and prayed: "Dear Lord, send us Manna from heaven!"

Nevertheless, I pressed on: "So I'm not missing the column because of the malaria?"

"In a way, yes." Shuttleworth admitted. "You were simply hospitalised at the wrong moment. You were just unlucky. It could happen to any of us. We've all had malaria, me, Calvert, Lentaine, even Wingate."

"Then it can only be because I'm thirty-eight." I said. "I'm too old to go in. I've been written off." "Nonsense!" Shuttleworth dismissed the accusation. He got up and patted me on the back. "Man for man, Berkovitz," he said, "you're still as good as anyone in the whole battalion."

Chapter 20

I'll never forget that last Christmas at Orcher in December 1943. It's one of those indelible wartime memories that has taken its place permanently alongside Macpherson on the Britannic and Wingate's arrival in Cawnpore. It wasn't any one spectacular incident I remember so vividly, but the whole boozy evening when I seemed to be developing second sight. My friend Jock Hamilton, the Adjutant's batman, had managed to get hold of a couple of bottles of gin, and we'd detached ourselves from the main body of merrymakers and were sitting quietly, legs outstretched, on some bamboo, happily trying to get ourselves sozzled. Everybody had had more than enough, but there were no fighting drunks. What you'd hear all night was mainly snatches of songs, jokes and much laughter. A young Chindit, Alan Crooks, I'd known in the Fusiliers, making his way unsteadily from the bog with a bottle clutched in one hand, gave us a sickly smile of recognition as he passed us and moved across to join his mates. Through the liquor haze, his face dissolved into a grinning skull, the skin simply falling away, leaving just teeth embedded in the bone structure. I shuddered.

Jock must have noticed.

"What's up?" he asked.

"Did you see young Crooksy?" I replied.

"Of course I did," he said. "What do you think I am, drunk?"

"He's a dead man, Jock, dead," I said.

"Dead? Dead drunk you mean?" relied Jock.

"No Jock, Crooksy's a dead man. Just plain dead," I said.

Jock shrugged his shoulders. "We're all dead men." Jock held out the bottle. "Drink up Sam. We'll all be dead men a long time."

I took another swig from the bottle, but I knew Crooksy's number was up. He went out in the New Year with one of the columns, got in a night fight with some Japanese and was shot in the throat.

He was sent back to Command Post HQ where, after dark, you had to identify yourself correctly or they wouldn't let you in the stockade. A young officer challenged him: he couldn't reply, so the officer shot him dead. It was Wingate's first law of the jungle: 'At night, if you see or hear someone moving towards you and he doesn't answer your challenge, you shoot – to kill.'

Jock and I sat in amiable congress. Of Scots parentage, born in Oldham, he was a hard-bitten, long service regular. He'd been at one time made up to Sergeant, busted for being drunk and had worked his way back to Corporal, then busted again for being AWOL. Now he was, like me, a private soldier, and also took care of the Adjutant's personal needs.

Jack was just above average height, but looked quite short, being built like the back of a barn with the biggest shoulders I've ever seen on anyone. He was capable and intelligent, had a sense of humour and a heart of gold. He was always arranging for me to share the Adjutant's tea, when the officer wasn't there, of course. That was my weakness. The only thing that would have tempted me to apply for a commission was a couple of cups of tea handed me by a batman first thing in the morning before breakfast.

In billets at Cawnpore, there was no need to be an officer. We were serviced by a small army of Indian camp followers. The NAAFI Wallah picked up my net curtains just after six in the morning and started shaving me while I slept. Then the Char Wallah came in and brought my first cups of tea of the day, steaming hot and strong. The Dhobi Wallah called to collect the laundry and did all my washing for a small fee. The Dhursi Wallah repaired my clothes and darned my socks and a small boy, one of the Wallah's sons, was detailed for a pittance to do my brass so that everything metal on my equipment shone, especially on sentry duty.

After we'd finished the routine army day beginning at six o'clock, we'd sit up in the billet till about ten, chatting generalities, smoking and playing cards, with the Char Wallah hovering around within earshot in the alleyway or on the verandah. I didn't even have to raise my voice with: "Char Wallah, make piala char,": he was there at my side with the tea, anticipating my request. The result was that I got through at least six cups of tea and wads every evening and, at the end of the week, I had to hand over most of my pay to him. With what he got from my mates, the Char Wallah certainly ended up the week with more money than I did.

I was always broke, but I enjoyed it. There must be a masochistic as well as a sybaritic streak in my makeup, possibly inherited from one of the near Asiatic tribesmen who'd swept through the southern Rumanian villages, murdering and raping my medieval Jewish ancestors and scattering their seed among the terrified women. I sometimes fancied it would have suited me to be a Pasha, sitting cross-legged on a velvet cushion, being fed with endless cups of sweet Turkish coffee and piles of small sticky cakes, and occasionally beckoning one of my houris over for a quick tickle.

Drink seemed to have no effect on the hard-living Jock, but I could feel myself becoming quite maudlin and misty-eyed over the departure of my friend. I felt an overwhelming tenderness and brotherly love towards him, which had nothing to do with all those gallons of tea we'd also shared.

Oddly too, these noble sentiments were tinged with jealousy because I wasn't going in and he was. I put my hand on his arm and told him how genuinely sorry I was not to be going in with him.

"Don't be sorry, Sam." he said. "I'm not going in either."

I was shocked. "You're joking Jock!"

He shook his head. "I don't joke about such things. I'm fed up with the bloody war. I'm fed up with the bloody British army. I've already had a basinful in France and here the Japanese are also wiping the floor with us. I've had enough. I've got a bint just outside Delhi. I'll be able to hole up with her there. Her people would look after me."

"They'll catch you." I said. "If they don't shoot you it'll be jankers. Maybe for years."

"So what. At least I'll come out and still be alive."

"Jock,' I entreated him. "Don't talk bloody nonsense. You've <u>got</u> to go in!"

He could have retorted it was very nice for me to talk, but I wasn't going in myself. He knew, however, that I wasn't scared, just as I knew he wasn't scared either. He simply wasn't very keen on this phase of operations, which meant helping the Burmese.

"Why," he asked, "should we go in to get the Japanese out of Burma? Without earlier Burmese help, the Japanese would never have got us out of the sodding place. Let the Burmese get 'em out themselves. Let 'em stew in their own juice. I'm not going."

Suddenly the argument became of tremendous importance. I felt terribly involved. It was a matter of life and death for me as if my own continued existence depended on Jock joining the column. "Jock, my dear old Jock," I beseeched him, "You've got to go. They're our chaps, your own mates in your own section. There's a hole in the line if you're not there. The section ain't complete without you. It's a matter of personal friendships. Your *esprit de corps*, your loyalties to the battalion, to the Adjutant. That boy leans on you for help more than anyone else in the Company.

Jock," I urged him again. "You must go in!"

He didn't say anything for a moment. I half expected him to break out with: "Sod the Adjutant and sod the battalion and sod you too!," but he just gave a sheepish grin and finally said "Okay Sam, I'll go."

"Wait a minute, Jock," I said. "Here's a silver rupee. It's a bit bent but still legal tender. Now you owe me a chip. As a Scot you won't rest till you've paid me back, and as a Jew I won't rest till I get it. We won't let a rupee come between us and it'll be a token, a bond that'll bring you back."

We shook hands and drank some more gin and finally I ambled off to my tent in a state of muzzy euphoria. My friend Jock marched out in February with Major Shuttleworth's column, due to rendezvous with other columns in North Burma 150 miles behind the Japanese lines at a large, quickly constructed but easily dismantled strongpoint code-named White City. This was to be their HQ under the command of Mike Calvert, by then a Brigadier. From there, Wingate's plan was to interfere with all Japanese troop movements to the North, where the Japanese were mounting their campaign for the invasion of India.

Shuttleworth's column began to move. They staged a couple of successful ambushes, blew up some railway culverts and kept popping up from nowhere to harass the enemy before they disappeared back into the jungle.

Jock, I heard, was loving it. He found the excitement and action a tonic. Unhappily, sometime in March, he fell ill along with several others and as Shuttleworth couldn't allow anything to hamper his mobility, the Major decided to send them back to White City where they could receive appropriate medical attention or be airlifted back to India for hospitalisation if required. Half a dozen sick men with an armed escort of two Chindits, also in need of care but not so badly, began the long walk back to White City. On the second day, while they were bivouacking for the night, a Japanese patrol ambushed them, cut the whole lot to pieces with bayonets and smashed in their faces to unrecognisable pulp. The Fusilier who told me about it said Jock was only identified by the massive width of his shoulders.

I was saddened and distressed to hear about it of course, but not for long. In the army there's no time to linger over misfortunes in the field, even to our nearest and dearest. That's life – and death. That's cold, sober fact. In fiction, Jock would have been identified not by his shoulders but by a bent rupee amongst his meagre belongings.

The Chindits, after Wingate disappeared from the scene around this time, had to suspend whatever operations they were engaged on. The American general, 'Vinegar Joe' Stilwell, his nickname reflecting his sour demeanour and lack of tact, needed help and, at his insistence, all the columns were sent in to attack the Japanese lines of communication. Along with General Stilwell, the army in India was never all that keen on the Chindit effort or, for that matter, the unpredictable Wingate, and was preparing to mount the 1945 campaign to dislodge the Japanese with a seaborne assault. They had the ships, the sailors, the soldiers and airplanes, and didn't want to go through the jungle at all. They occupied Rangoon swiftly and successfully in 1945, but the fact remains that much of what Generals Slim and Mountbatten were able to achieve later was basically due to Wingate clearing North Burma. He made the area untenable for the Japanese and enabled the 14th Army to position itself to take Mytella after the savage and bloody battle of the Infal Plain. Thus, the Chindit conception, which began as a thunderingly good idea, fizzled out in an unheeded whimper. A lot of our most expert men died in tactics for which they were never fully trained. On balance, however, I felt it worth the effort and sacrifices entailed and, in the long run, the Chindits left a legacy from which our latter-day commandos and SAS men have benefited greatly.

I rejoined my unit in Lucknow, where I found the 10th battalion Lancashire Fusiliers and the 1st battalion had been merged because of casualties. A lot of time-expired blokes had gone home, a number of them had died and many had been killed. When I came in from the air base, I was made up to Corporal without any fuss and put in charge of ammunition.

We went to Dehra Dun from there, to build up our strength, because everyone was coming down with malaria. I'd had, in the interim, a bout of amoebic dysentery too, not very pleasant, but I had recovered well. Dehra Dun, six thousand feet up, is relatively cool at night. From there you can see the foothills of the white crowned Himalayas and Masuri, the summer station of the Lancashire Fusiliers in peacetime. The soldiers used to holiday there with their families before the war.

We stayed in Dehra Dun for a month and then returned to Lucknow for garrison duties. Standing in the lorry going to the station in Dehra Dun, I allowed a little cooling wind to blow on me. That did it. In the train, I began to get weak, wobbled and fell asleep. When we got to Lucknow next morning I woke up and tried to leave the train, and collapsed yet again with malaria. I spent the next day, Christmas Eve, and the following two weeks, in Lucknow Hospital.

The diversity in character and outlook of my comrades always surprised me. We had aboard the Britannic a nice, inoffensive-looking bloke called Gregory, whom I'd known at Colchester, and when we got to Durban he jumped ship. He'd met a pretty girl ashore and she'd persuaded him to stay. When Macpherson called the roll on board after we had cast off, there were three men missing, Gregory amongst them. Our CO was shocked. One of them had been in a fight, got drunk and turned up eventually some months later; Gregory and another man really had done a bunk.

After we arrived at Bombay, an officer from our company was sent back to South Africa for a specialist course. He hired a taxi at the dockside and got the shock of his life when he saw that the driver was Gregory. Instead of getting him to drive direct to the Army camp, he told him to turn left and made him stop at the nearest police station. There, he took Gregory by the scruff of the neck and dragged him inside. "Hold this man in jail till the next trooper comes in," the Officer said. "I'll be on it and I'll take him back with me."

Gregory was put on punishment for six months, but it didn't bother him and, in due course, he settled down and turned out to be a good soldier, ending up as a full sergeant with a Military Medal to add to his campaign ribbons. At the time he crossed my path in Lucknow, he was only a Corporal, like me, and we were detailed to pick up another Corporal in Bombay who also had deserted and take him to Dehra Dun.

We drew our pay and expenses and picked the deserter up in Bombay. We got him on the train, keeping an eye on him all the time, as he was known to be a bit of a tearaway, and for the next couple of days he was under our strict surveillance, even when he went to the lavatory. At Delhi, we lodged the Corporal in the Red Fort and informed the police that we would pick him up in the morning.

We signed in at a very nice camp for squaddies, one of the best I had ever been in, with its own large swimming pool. Unfortunately, we visited the Lakshmi Race Track where we lost all our cash, including the ration money. What were we to do about supper? The morning was no problem, as we could get breakfast at the Fort, but both of us needed a good nosh-up right away or we'd go to bed hungry. There was nothing for it but to try and get some money from a sympathetic squaddie. We walked past the railway station where we'd be most likely to meet soldiers and spotted a young squaddie with a rather pale face. You can tell how much time a man's been here by the colour of his complexion. Gregory and I were both a deep, dark red, but this chap looked positively anaemic. He wore a big, old-fashioned toupee that alone branded him as one of the new boys because, after a while here, you got the Gurkha hat, and his shorts were freshly laundered and too long. I said to Gregory, "He's our man. Let me do the talking." We walked over to him and I explained the situation, that we were skint and needed a couple of rupees for food, and could he loan us the money?

"Certainly," he said, without hesitation. "Two rupees? Is that enough?"

"Plenty," I replied. "It's only for supper tonight and breakfast in the morning."

When he handed over the two chips, we both thanked him profusely. An ordnance man, he told us he was being posted to Calcutta and before he left, I asked him his name.

"Sam Berkovitz," he said.

It sounded quite incredible. At first, I couldn't believe my ears, and asked him to repeat it. But it was Sam Berkovitz all right. Two British soldiers with the same unpronounceable foreign name meeting up in, of all places, Delhi. He even came from an area I know well, East Mansions, off Whitechapel Road, a big block of flats later to earn the unwelcome distinction of being demolished by the last V2 rocket to hit London. When I met this Sam again after the war and we had a drink together, he told me the rocket had wiped out most of his family. Amazingly, there was yet a third Sam Berkovitz in our theatre of operations. When I came home, some people were surprised to find I was still alive. This third Sam Berkovitz had been killed in action in the Far East and many of my acquaintances had thought it was me.

Just as we were settling in again at Lucknow, we suddenly got orders to move to Allahabad, up in the United Provinces. We went to a big camp there but I have no recollection of doing anything at all in Allahabad. Then, one day a notice went up on the board: 'Parade Detail. One hundred men, one NCO Detail for service at Comilla.' Comilla was the base camp for the 14th Army in Burma. This army with its tanks had crossed the Irawadi, but hadn't yet reached Mytella. Mandalay had been captured by the British, Stilwell's Americans and Chinese had taken Michener, and things generally were hotting up.

It dawned on me that this detail must be it. I had spent nearly four years waiting to go in. I was now 38 and, with any luck, could celebrate my 39th birthday, only days away, in Comilla. Musing on this, I noticed the Adjutant walking across from his tent – we were all living under canvas then – towards HQ. Forgetful of channels and mindful only of my pressing needs, I doubled over to him and asked permission to speak. I poured out my woes. I told him I was the only NCO in the unit who hadn't been into Burma. I wanted to make the record straight. I wanted to go in with the 100 men.

Evidently my plea didn't fall on deaf ears. Next morning it was up on orders: a detail with the names of a hundred men for Comilla and Corporal Berkovitz. S. top of the list. It took us three days to pack and we were off on the first leg of our journey, by train. I didn't manage to make Comilla for my 39th birthday. I celebrated it with two fried eggs, toast, and a large pot of tea in the Sahib's Rest Room at Mogul Serai, a tiny one-track station *en route*.

The train chugged on till we reached Gallighat, where we spent the day. Then we boarded a boat and moved alongside the winding, Brahmaputra river until finally we reached Comilla. I marched the men in and saw the Warrant Officer in charge. "Here we are." I announced. "One hundred men and myself safe and sound. No sick, no wounded, no-one scarpered on the way. All present and correct. They're all yours, Sar'nt Major."

He ticked off the names and thanked me and I went outside with a sergeant to allot the men their billets. I'd imagined, once we'd got to Comilla, that we'd just about have time to change our socks before being rushed off to the Front. Not so. Two weeks later, we were still at Comilla, lounging about the camp, eating, sleeping and simply making a pretence at odd drills. I was beginning to get a bit worried. With the American Navy blowing the Japanese out of the water all over the Pacific and our own boys making much headway in Burma, I was afraid the war might be over by the time I had a chance to join in.

I went to see the RSM. "What's happening, Sar'nt Major?" I asked. "There's supposed to be an urgent need for reinforcements, yet here we are sitting around in Comilla eating our arses off and nothing happening."

"There's plenty happening, Corporal." he said, "but at the moment it doesn't concern you. I don't mean that in a nasty way; I'm not telling you off. What I mean is that we can't move with replacements until we know what's wanted and where. Possibly there's a quiet period at the moment, possibly regrouping, possibly any of a hundred and one things. But most likely it's a matter of plain logistics, how many aeroplanes are available, who should go first - urgent stores or men - or do they both go in together? Rest assured though, as soon as we hear something definite, your detachment will be on its way and, if it's any consolation to you, and for your ears only, their departure can't be any more than a day or two delayed."

I was just about to leave the office when he motioned me to remain. "By the way, Berkovitz," he said. "I've had a word with the CO and you'll be staying here with me."

He must have noted the look of dismay on my face. "What's up?" he asked. "I thought you'd be pleased." I drew a deep breath. "Sar'nt Major," I blurted out. "I'm sorry. I'm not. I know I ought to be grateful to you for wanting to keep me here, but I have to get to Burma. Believe it or not, I've been travelling four years to get there and now I'm within spitting distance, I can't stay behind. I've trained four years to become a fighting soldier and I want to fight. Every NCO in the unit has seen some action except me. I'm 39 and liable to get another dose of malaria any day now, especially if I hang around here. There's a mosquito also hanging around specifically to bite me and I'll finish up dead in a hospital bed in India instead of fighting in Burma."

"Take it easy Corporal," said the RSM "Of course, I won't keep you here if you're so set on going, but even if you stayed awhile, you'd still get your fill of fighting. The Japanese are wily, obstinate buggers. They won't give in easily. The war isn't over yet by a long chalk and it won't be till we get to Tokyo."

A couple of days later, several Dakotas flew in to the base, one earmarked for us, though it could only take 60 men, plus some vital equipment. The RSM, now very sympathetic, called me into the company office and gave me a choice of the men I wanted to take along with me. They were a pretty good bunch of lads and any of them would do to make up the number, apart from three privates whom I considered quite unsuitable for front line duty. One was a good, willing youth who was so thick his rifle was always going off. Wherever he was, there would suddenly be a shot. Another suffered badly from nerves: in a tight corner, that could be contagious, possibly fatal. The third was an obvious homosexual: he was in the Lancashire Fusiliers and a Chindit, but he didn't serve at the air base and was probably employed in the rear echelon at Jhani. I knew my hero, Alexander, was a homosexual and I had a pretty good idea a couple of our own senior officers were too, but I had an immense admiration for them as hard men and brilliant dedicated soldiers. This Private, though, could be a disruptive influence in the ranks at awkward moments, so I allowed my own prejudices to influence my judgement as to his suitability for the draft.

After breakfast, I marched my men down to the airstrip and we got in the plane, where we sat down on wooden benches ranged lengthwise down the body, so disposing ourselves and personal baggage in reasonable comfort for the short journey ahead. There we sat. And sat. The sun hung suspended overhead in glaring splendour. The air sizzled and fairly crackled with heat. It brought to mind the lyrics of Noel Coward's song 'Mad dogs and Englishmen go out in the midday sun.' He could have added 'or sit in aeroplanes', or, worst of all, 'huddle in full kit on Dakotas'.

Don't think I'm running down the Dakota. It's an admirable workhorse. I swore by their safety and reliability. I'd loaded them dozens of times to drop Colonel Lord's manna on the Chindit columns in the jungle below. Those solid metal plates could stand any air stress or strain and accommodated when necessary an extra 500 pounds of stores above the approved load without any bother at all. But stationary, with the sun relentlessly beating down and the atmosphere growing more stifling with every breath, the Dakota's sound construction lost its attraction, by turning into an oven, thus sealing in the heat.

After an hour or so, the pilot got in. But still no movement. No sound of revving up engines. I went to the cockpit to enquire what was happening and when, and was informed that we were going to Mytella, about three or four hundred miles inside Burma. We couldn't take off, however, till we got their okay. They'd have to send up some fighters for a couple of sweeps to make sure no Japanese planes were in the area before we took off, although there was always the chance of some rogue Zero fighter lurking behind cloud cover. With its speed and manoeuvrability, the Zero could swoop down before we even noticed and cut us up with its 22mm cannon in ten seconds flat.

I got back on my seat and the wooden form grew more uncomfortable by the minute. There was no let-up in the heat. I began to sweat and then started to drink from the chagall, a kind of artificial skin made from canvas, which somehow keeps the water cool. I drank just moderate mouthfuls at first but, as the hours passed by, I gulped copiously until I'd got through about eight pints. As I ingested the water, it seemed to come straight out through my skin. I could have been back at Scheftchik's Russian vapour baths in Brick Lane with my pal Hymie, any Friday afternoon, sweating in a similarly uncomfortable posture on another such wooden bench.

Suddenly, the too familiar symptoms assailed me. I felt as though that warm collar was tightening round my neck again. I began to shiver. I was hot and cold alternately. Good Lord! I thought. Not malaria. Not here. Not now, when I'm so close to going in. Not four years of harsh self-discipline going down the drain! I shut my eyes, praying desperately that this was not going to happen to me.

"You okay, Corp?" asked one of the soldiers seated opposite. He was a fisherman from St. Annes, near Blackpool, who had volunteered because his mates were in the Fusiliers and he thought the army would be more exciting than the war at sea. "You look about the same colour as our boiled lobsters back home," he commented. 'You will soon have steam coming out of your ears."

"It's nothing." I said, willing myself to stay conscious, to stay alive. I was sure that if I flaked out, was carried off the plane and missed this flight, I'd be dead. "I'm only a bit hot. Be better when we're on the move."

Miraculously, the fit of shivering passed, the constriction round my neck eased and eventually the Dakota took off with me on board, rumpled, hot and only a little the worse for wear. We landed about an hour and three quarters later on the tarmac at Mytella. I was wearing ammunition boots with every justification. I was finally in combat.

Chapter 21

Several armoured personnel carriers were drawn up on the tarmac after our Dakota landed. We were met by a tall, young subaltern with a worried expression, who kept consulting some document in his field map case and jotting down figures. He could have been plotting a reference or checking our destination or ascertaining whether our numbers tallied with his movement orders, or maybe he was just trying to look busy to impress us. Meantime, we clambered on board the waiting vehicles with all our gear and were moved to a concealed roadway at the edge of the airfield. After a while a jeep drew up and a grey-haired Captain jumped out. He immediately began to confer with the young subaltern, with lots of prodding at the map case until they finally seemed to agree. The Lieutenant saluted and the officer drove off. The young subaltern then came up to the leading carrier where, as senior soldier, I was sitting next to the driver, thumped on the door and yelled: "Okay, lads. On your way!"

I was still feeling a bit queasy, but my mental exhilaration more than compensated for my poor physical condition. I'd arrived in Burma. I was in and at last I was going to see some action. We were now part of the Border Regiment at the disposal of the Company Commander, who was sending us down to join their reconnaissance group called the Reivers – Border Bandits – which had suffered a lot of casualties and was being made up to strength in the field. At the moment, the Reivers were encamped at Tongu, some thirty miles distant and that was where our little convoy was headed.

Our driver, quite garrulous for one of those dour northerners, had been with the Borderers for some time and proudly described the points of interest *en route*: the remains of an odd truncated pagoda, part of a reclining Buddha, but mainly he showed us enormous bomb craters where ammunition dumps had been exploded and the ruins of demolished strongpoints. Only a week or so back, there had been quite severe fighting in this area and we saw what looked like large rag dolls hanging limply from trees. They were Japanese snipers, explained our Reiver. They were told to fight to the death. And they did. They had to. They were tied to the branches. When our boys spotted them, they whistled up the air-force and our Typhoons blasted the hell out of the trees and the snipers.

Even so, our guide commented, these 1945 Japanese weren't the swaggering all-conquering Japanese of 1942. The '42 invaders were proud and happy to die for the Emperor under any circumstances and would never surrender, whatever the odds. Now they were on the run, they had learned a little circumspection. When they were surrounded and forced to give in, they now submitted to the indignity of laying down their arms without too much argument. I was resolved that if any Japanese I encountered were still happy to die for the Emperor, I'd be delighted to spread as much happiness as possible.

When we got to our camp near a little village not too far from Tongu, it was quite dark. In the tropics, sunset is no big deal. It doesn't stretch out like our own lingering twilight back home. At night, it's quite light until the sun drops below the horizon and then it becomes pitch black in about two minutes flat. There's no great sunrise either. Everything happens in seconds. It's dark, and suddenly there's a patch of red in the East and in less than five minutes it's broad daylight.

We climbed down from the carriers, got our stuff together and waited for someone in authority to tell us what to do. The RSM came along after a while with a sheaf of documents in his hand and, looking at us realised, even in the dark, that we were completely exhausted. "All right." he said, switching off his torch. "Finish off your rations and bed down where you can. There won't be any work for you tonight. But no lights. No smoking. Parade at 6 a.m. sharp."

Thankfully, we ate what was left of our food. I gave mine to our Reiver driver who'd shown on the journey that he had an insatiable appetite, and settled down for the night with the others under the parked vehicles. I hadn't been lying down for long when I was suddenly gripped by a terrible pain in my stomach. I could swear my large intestine had become knotted into a reef, and was twisting itself right. It was the father and mother of bellyaches. I cursed myself as an idiot for allowing my thirst to get the better of me. One of the first things they taught us in acclimatisation at Rawalpindi was that, when you're hot and sweaty in the tropics, and running a bit of a temperature, cool down a little before you let yourself loose on the water, otherwise you could be in for a bout of colic, or worse. My trouble was, as I dragged my tortured body from under the carrier to relieve myself, that I felt it may be much worse than colic.

Unbuckling my belt as I staggered towards some low bushes about ten yards away, I dropped my trousers and squatted behind them. Before I could get on with the job, a shadowy figure loomed out of the darkness.

"Halt. Who goes there?" came a challenge.

"Friend!" I returned hurriedly. "Friend!" I rose to my feet, one hand clutching my pants, the other in the air. "Don't shoot. Friend! Don't shoot!" I pleaded.

"Password!" the sentry repeated grimly.

I heard the ominous click of a rifle bolt jerked into the groove and I panicked. In that fraction of a second I felt what it was like to be shot dead by mistake, like Crooksy when he couldn't answer. My voice rose hysterically. I had to stop this terrible miscarriage of justice.

"I don't know the password! The RSM didn't tell us. We came too late. I'm from the Lancashire Fusiliers."

The man with the gun started to laugh. It enraged me still further. "For Chrissake then, shoot, if you don't believe me!" With my free hand I jabbed at my stomach. "Right here. Shoot. You'll be doing me a favour!"

"Why, it's old Berko," the sentry chuckled. "Thought I recognised that cockney whine. Know it anywhere. The only Sherwood Forester from Whitechapel. I'm Bernie Wilks from 13th battalion."

His voice changed as if he was giving me an order. "Carry on crapping, Sam, but don't wander too far out or you might get a Japanese bayonet up your arse!"

Vastly relieved in more senses than one, after uninterruptedly completing my business, I made my way back to sleeping quarters. My exhausted men hadn't heard a thing, but the driver was wide awake.

"Lucky escape, mate." he said, turning on his side.

It was more than lucky, I thought, it was bloody miraculous. Now it was past midnight. Despite all the alarms and excursions of the journey and having suffered the indignity of being caught with my trousers down, my first day in Burma was complete. It would have been an ending ironic enough for O. Henry if, after all my struggles to get here, I'd have perished on my first day, without firing a bullet, earning me the miserable epitaph – 'Got shot shitting!'

My own lucky deliverance made me reflect how much luck determines even the results of wars. I didn't regard war as a very profound business at all. Clausewitz, Napoleon, Wellington, Caesar, Liddell Hart, and all my other friends in the Whitechapel Library had woven a mystique around what was simply a problem of physical displacement. Whether you do it with an atom bomb, a bayonet charge, or an armoured corps attack, war is still basically a matter of shoving the other bloke out of the way, and having a bit of luck with it, like Napoleon, who should've been killed a dozen times in his early campaigns. Napoleon was very lucky, but he didn't seem to learn from his mistakes. In the end he was defeated by Wellington because he made the same errors as in his previous battles and, at Waterloo, luck was on Wellington's side.

With the tumult in my stomach stilled, only one thing remained to make it a perfect day: getting my baptism of fire. As if in answer to my pent-up longings, a gun with a sharp bark opened up quite close, firing a round every few minutes.

"One of ours?" I enquired.

"No, one of theirs," said the Reiver. "It's a Jap 88 mm. Now it's one of ours. We captured it. Good bit of artillery. Plenty of bite. It'll stop for a bit, start again, and go on like this, shooting off the old stock all night."

"All night? – Why?" I asked.

"Just to remind 'em we're on their tails. And to keep the buggers awake."

"Us too?"

"Not us," he said. 'We know where it's coming from and when it's going off. We're used to it." He yawned and in a moment was snoring gently. I could feel myself drifting off as well, soothed by the lullaby of the Jap 88 and I soon fell asleep happy and gloriously alive and in the war at last.

Next day, the RSM put me in charge of a section comprising seven old hands from his recce unit plus three of the men I'd brought along with me to make up. We seemed to mix pretty well although, with me in charge, it didn't seem to go down so well with the Lance Corporal named Rivers, who thought he was hard-done-by and it should have been him with his two stripes in charge. However, there was a cigarette issue and, as I did not smoke, my 20 fags were impartially distributed, two for each man. That, more than my mature years, established my seniority in the section, although the very much younger Rivers probably had a stronger claim to leadership, as he'd slogged successfully through the first couple of hundred miles of Burma already.

At the end of May, Rangoon had been captured by an amphibious assault and the Imperial Japanese Army was in retreat on all fronts. The Reivers were astride the Road to Mandalay where, as Kipling has it, 'the flying fishes play'. The Road, built by the British in the 19th century, was about 400 miles long and ran from Mandalay to Rangoon. We identified places not by names, but by the milestones: for example, Milestone 60, where I had my first real brush with the enemy, was 60 miles from Rangoon and about 340 from Mandalay. We were now chasing the Japanese all the way, but had quite a job getting to grips with them. They'd been ordered to get off the Road, cross over and try and get into Siam, where the remnants of their defeated Burmese Army were concentrated. The Reivers would move into different places and patrol the area. We'd hear that the Japanese were at a certain spot so we would reconnoitre the area but usually found nothing. We were at Pegu, about 40 miles from Rangoon, when we got news of the victorious amphibious assault on the city, and were sent back along the Mandalay Road to a place called Pembigon. We made this our base for a while and mounted our patrols from there. Pembigon is on the Sitang River, not a waterway of good repute for the British Army. We got a thrashing there in 1942 when a bridge, blown up too soon, caused a lot of our men on the other side of the river to be completely surrounded and practically annihilated. The local Burmese were also great opportunists. In 1942, they helped the Japanese to eject the British army from Burma. However, after a couple of years under Japanese domination, these same Burmese were very glad to see us coming back.

From Pembigon, we began to circle the area. Suddenly, we heard there was a concentration of Japanese troops at Milestone 60. Off we dashed to Milestone 60, arriving there in the evening and prepared to attack it in the morning. It was reported to be very strongly held because a previous patrol had gone in and been heavily engaged by the Japanese still there.

We took up our position that evening about a mile from the village, which was really only a couple of long winding streets with houses on stilts, surrounded by a stockade of trees. The Burmese always built their villages inside a shielding area of trees to protect their livestock from animal predators and human bandits. We infiltrated the area and formed a big semicircle round it. Then we whistled up the RAF and Typhoons flew over to deal with any snipers in the trees. A dozen fighters singly and in pairs zoomed in and, for an hour, hammered those trees with their cannon until the trunks and foliage looked as devastated as if they'd been in the path of a raging tornado.

With the earth still shuddering from the cannon fire and roar of aeroplane engines, our artillery opened up and we went in under a creeping barrage. A dense curtain of shells dropped a hundred yards in front of us, so close overhead I could feel their heat on my face. On we marched, through that first hundred yards and then stood down. The barrage lifted and we went forward another hundred yards. That's how it went on, stopping and starting for several hours till we'd covered the mile that took us right into the village street.

I was hungry and tired. I knew my men must be suffering too. Fatigue is the soldier's worst enemy. If he is hungry and hot, as well as tired, he doesn't give a damn what happens to him. For myself, I was gasping and sweating, but still mentally in control. The section was closing up. I was supposed to be in the middle and not at the end, and humans, being what they are, they'd begun to knot together. "If you get into a bunch," I whispered to those around me, "one burst from a machine gun can take the whole bloody lot of you. Thin out! Thin out!"

Cautiously, we entered the village. Nothing moved. No-one fired at us. As we went in, I passed the entrance to the forward bunkers. Automatically I fired two shots in the hole. 'One for Jock, and one for young Crooksy,' I said to myself. That was the sum total of military activity inside the village at Milestone 60. The Japanese, of course, had long gone.

We stayed in the area for a couple of days, then went on to liberate another village. Our trek was over such rough country that my boots came off in the mud. That's what a paddy is: damp, dark, marvellously glutinous earth, that can grow a crop of rice in six weeks, although there's a lot of backbreaking work that goes into the harvesting. There were a couple of miles of this paddy, life for the village but purgatory for us, leaving us exhausted. We found the village entirely surrounded by paddy fields. To get in we had to walk along the booms. There was no lateral movement at all, only linear movement that meant if there were a couple of enemy machine gunners properly posted there'd be no future in it for us. Our Captain looked at the paddy and scratched his head. "I don't know what to do," he said, finally. 'We'll make an attempt, anyhow.'

We started along the booms but machine guns opened up and we fell back. The officer called in the gunners and they fired a hundred or more shells right over the approaches to the village. Again, we got up and tried to move forward, and again the machine guns opened up. Apparently, our artillery hadn't had the desired effect. In this terrain, unless a shell scores a direct hit, it explodes with a plop in the soggy earth and does little damage to anyone well dug in. It was obviously a job for mortars, our Captain decided, as they explode a little above the ground, but as we didn't have any, he called the whole thing off and we trudged back over another couple of miles of clinging paddy to the trucks and drove back to camp. Next morning, the heavy mortars went in. They did their work well but, when we hauled ourselves across the paddy later on, we found plenty of devastation in the village, but no Japanese troops.

Back at Pembigon, scouts reported there were some Japanese in another village close by. The Company Commander called me in and told me there weren't so many, so it would only be an attack in Company strength. "Take out your section," he said. "I've got a guide here for you. Go all the way round the back. I'll put in a diversionary attack up front, and you can outflank the Japs without any bother."

I called my section out and we were joined by this cocky little Burmese who would act as guide. We made an early start because it would be footslogging all the way. Not only would we have to navigate the ubiquitous paddy, but go through elephant grass as well, taller than a man's head, so our guide said.

Before we moved out, I warned the guide: "If we've got to go round the back, we mustn't be seen. The point about an ambush is that it's always unexpected. I want us to march there and get round the village. I'll go a bit out of my way if you like. I'll walk an extra mile, even two miles, but we've got to get there without being observed."

Our guide grinned and nodded. He understood quite a bit of English. "Leave it to me." he said. He led us across closed country, plenty of bushes, forest, trees and elephant grass, all excellent cover, and then brought us out into open paddy with, straight ahead of us, the village houses not a mile away. I pulled him up sharp. "This is no good. No good at all. We can't make an ambush if they know we're here!"

"No. They don't see you." he replied. "Road is curved. You be alright," he assured me.

I'm a map-reader and I know contours. I could see the village and I knew they could see me, but I was under orders to go there. The guide led us into the grass again, and we followed. I gave instructions to close-up – you can lose someone there very easily. He need only be a couple of yards away and you can't see him, the grass is so thick. It was heavy going too and the coarse grass cut into your skin with every step. Suddenly, we came out on a track and, about three hundred yards away, we could see the village. At first, I thought this damned, smiling villain had sold us out, but I reflected it wouldn't be of much benefit to him if he did because, where he was in the van, he'd be the first to be killed. I was right behind him, so I continued marching, with the rest of the column following in single file.

A Hotchkiss machine gun broke the silence, a sound like a treadle-operated sewing machine badly in need of lubrication. We had obviously been spotted. The ambush was a washout and we'd be lucky to get out of it alive. I gave the order: "Fall back." and we retreated to the safety of the elephant grass. About twenty yards inside, I gathered the patrol around me, all of us squatting on our haunches. I told them to form a square with a minimum of movement, and stay put until I ordered otherwise. Meantime, the Hotchkiss was searching us out, but the bullets were high, rising slightly as they skimmed through the grass.

The Captain's original battle plan was that, after he'd put in his frontal attack to flush out the Japanese, we would finish them off with our 303 Enfields. He would then fire a single rocket to recall us. Well, he'd put in his attack, but the Japanese had seen him off and he realised that, without heavy mortars at least, it would be useless to continue the attack. Considering the unexpectedly large number of Japanese, it would have to be a full battalion attack the next day.

Heavy machine guns along with the heavy mortars as arranged, the Captain fired the recall rocket but in elephant grass all you can see is a little patch of sky directly overhead. The rocket went up a mile away, but none of us caught even a glimpse of it. We sat there and waited. I figured that, if the Japanese came in after us, we could still stage an ambush. But these were the Japanese of '45, not those of '42, meaning that, while they were still happy to die for the Emperor, they didn't feel obliged to rush so precipitously towards certain destruction.

We waited boxed up for two hours. My boys were getting restive as the day drew in. I was in two minds about staying longer or moving off without the recall rocket, which we didn't know had already gone off. The decision was made for me when a second machine gun opened up from a different direction and at a slightly different angle. Obviously, they'd spotted some movement and bullets were slicing through the grass uncomfortably close but, fortunately, still a little above our heads. I grabbed hold of our guide. "Get in front and lead us out," I told him. To the boys, I said: "Back out. Get going. Pull back." As they turned and ran, I faced in the general direction of the enemy and fired twice, mainly for moral effect, because there was nothing I could see in front of me but elephant grass.

We staggered out behind the guide, reformed and returned to camp. The Company Commander was very disgruntled when he got my report. Then he discovered something else had gone wrong. The man with our Bren gun had left it behind. "You don't seem to have handled your section very well," he observed. I was going to reply that he hadn't done all that marvellously with his own attack either. At least I'd extricated my men without any casualties, but I decided on discretion. It wouldn't do to fall out with a Company Commander, especially if you didn't know him very well. He wasn't like my sympathetic old officers from the Fusiliers and the Foresters, but a much younger, more unbending type. His face stiffened into a frown. "You know you're a Bren gun short?" he repeated.

I nodded. "Yes Sir."

"It has to be accounted for," he said. "I take a very dim view of this, Corporal Berkovitz. It's a very serious matter. I'll have to report it to the Colonel; it could even get as far as a Court of Inquiry." He looked at me closely. "There is an alternative, however."

"Like what?" I asked.

"Well, you can give up your stripes. That'll help pay for the gun. At least you'll know you were punished for the loss. Unfortunate, but there it is. It's up to you," he replied.

I didn't say anything, but I felt it was monstrous. I was seething. Kicking up a fuss because we were one gun short, when we'd lost hundreds, maybe thousands of guns in Singapore alone, not to mention the mass of equipment already dropped and lost to date in Burma. Besides, it wasn't my fault. I was leading my men out of danger and couldn't be held responsible for someone behind my back who panicked. Of course, I knew who it was. I'd put this bloke Wilkins in charge of the gun myself, and he was the last person I'd expect to lose his head.

A court of inquiry or even a Court Martial didn't worry me. I had the witnesses if required; nine men who knew exactly what had happened and whose evidence would certainly clear me. Then I remembered that Wilkins and four or five more of my men had served their time in India and were due to go home. They'd even been officially informed of this and really shouldn't have been out there with me chasing the Japanese at all. The period of service in this overseas theatre was now three years and eight months and Wilkins and the others had done over four years, and were months overdue. If they'd been in India, they'd be on their way home by now but, in the middle of Burma, there was no easy way to get them out. They were being doubly penalised already and I would only compound their troubles by making them wait for a Court of Inquiry to be set up and functioning.

"Well?" the Company Commander enquired after a while, "Think about it. You've no need to answer right away. Let me know what you've decided to do in the morning."

"I can tell you now, Sir," I said. "If it means there won't be a Court of Inquiry, I'll become a Private."

For a couple of days I was angry and sullen and felt aggrieved, until finally I accepted the situation. It had galled me after striving for more than four years to become an NCO to be reduced to the ranks because someone else had panicked. But, I reflected, it wasn't just someone else. All these men were family. I couldn't let them down. For four years, whenever I'd been posted into different units, they became my family so long as we stayed together and, when I moved, only the names changed.

I had an especially soft spot for Wilkins, anyway. When we were in the same barracks in Cawnpore, I was chosen to go to Bombay for a film the Indian Army Council were making, showing how representative soldiers from every area in Britain were faring in India. There were only two Londoners in my unit of the Lancashire Fusiliers and I, as the oldest, was chosen. When Wilkins remarked I didn't look too happy, I told him it was hard to be ecstatic when all I'd have for the seven days in Bombay would be my ration money and one week's pay. I thought no more about it and went to hand in my kit. When I returned for my spare shirts, I found forty rupees on the bed.

"What's this?" I asked.

"It's yours," someone said.

In the few minutes I'd been away, these boys, all pretty hard-up themselves, had had a whip round on my behalf. Here were forty rupees on the bed for which I hadn't asked, but was nevertheless very grateful. To this very day, I don't know who was responsible. All I know is they were my friends and family and Wilkins was one of them.

A film was shot in a little Bombay studio. A soldier got on a platform with a camera and was allowed one minute in which to send a message home to his family. Then he said "Now may I introduce Sam Berkovitz." I took his place for a minute and told my wife and son how well I was, how chirpy and full of beans. Then I called the next bloke, who came from the Old Kent Road, and so it went on.

My wife and child came down from Bishop Auckland to London when the War Office showed the film and, true to form, young Barry kicked up such a row when he saw his father on the screen that they had to show it for a second time. Bess wrote as well to tell me how fit I looked. She didn't know I was suffering from incipient dysentery. The minute before I went on I'd been to the lavatory and the minute after, I only just made it back. Altogether, I visited the Bombay Studio's toilet eighteen times during that morning's shooting.

My five men duly went home with a batch of other Indian time served men the following week. I saw them off on the lorry and, though British soldiers are not given over much to sentiment, they all shook me warmly by the hand before they mounted. They knew I'd taken the blame for them and appreciated it.

"We won't forget, Sam," said one. "You got us out of a sticky hole." Wilkins couldn't speak. He was choked up. He gave me a bear hug and his eyes filled with tears. He looked at me like my mute friend Pancho when I had to return him to his muleteer.

Chapter 22

When I lost my stripes, Rivers was made up to full Corporal and I became one of the section instead of its leader. But it didn't make any difference: we were still mates. He didn't try to pull rank with me and I didn't go out of my way to make trouble. As for our Captain, from my point of view I reckoned he'd been unnecessarily harsh, but he'd acted justly by the book. We were all governed by King's Regulations. Every once in a while, during a long, slack spell, the adjutant or our Company Commander would read us a section of King's Regulations and invite questions, the idea being to give us some notion of the rules that governed our lives. I found them quite interesting and even surprising in that the soldier had more rights than responsibilities.

The interpretation of King's Regulations was quite flexible as our Captain demonstrated when he tore off my two stripes, but I found them very reasonable in every way and I must say that, if you go by the rules, you must be mental or criminal to get into serious trouble with the army authorities, and they really leaned over backwards to help you with any personal problems.

The rank and file enjoyed a strange sort of democracy. No-one had a vote but, within the general framework of King's Regulations, each regiment had its own individual customs and was allowed its own way of running things.

Although I made no secret of my left-wing sympathies when I joined the army, I decided I wasn't going to be a barrack room lawyer. I found a lot of the men were Labour supporters and even some of the officers. One I got quite pally with when we discovered a common interest in history. His political stance was somewhere left of Trotsky, a hangover from his Cambridge days but, when the chips were down, he probably voted Tory, like the rest of his friends and relatives.

During my army career, I was only in four different battalions. Except for my posh Trotskyist friend, I never got to know any of the officers intimately. I only saw them on occasion and spoke to them rarely, but I was impressed with their high quality and that of the warrant officers, who must have been remarkable men. They'd dealt with soldiers all their lives and had come up from the ranks by their own efforts. To be an RSM in the pre-war army you had to be a quite exceptional person.

I was an orthodox soldier. I saluted the flag with pride. I used to walk across to the Cameronians to hear their pipers blow Retreat at six o'clock at night when we were in the jungle camp at Orcher. I liked the sound of the pipes and what it stood for. It may also have struck some tucked-away folk memory of my father's country, Rumania, where the pipes of Pan are popular and a primitive form of bagpipes is still played in rural areas. But it was undeniable that for hundreds of years the pipes were a significant feature of the British way of Army life.

In Lucknow I couldn't wait to get to the Residency to see the walls pockmarked with bullets and to go and stand where the defenders stood during its relief in 1857. And, naturally, I had to see the room where Flora Macdonald heard the pipes of Sir James Outram's relieving column several days before they actually reached the vicinity.

For a while at Orcher we had the South Staffs' with us. They were a proud, independent regiment who wouldn't allow Indians to have anything to do with their victualling. They had no native camp followers, only white cooks and white servants. Everything was done by their own men. They erected a big marquee and, at the end of the day, all the officers would march in wearing regimentals, and sit round the table and, after dinner, pass the port, the Colonel presiding at the head.

In the barracks, I never railed against the bosses, although most of the boys there were doubtless victims of the capitalist system. I was sure things could be improved, but I was against historical solutions to contemporary problems as advocated by orthodox Marxists. If I had nothing but admiration and respect for those above me, I had a tremendous feeling of warmth towards the rank and file, those ordinary working class chaps like myself and, living with them, my affection increased. They were funny, they were lively and they were generous although they had very little to be generous with. I shall never forget the sight of those forty rupees lying on my bed by the veranda and nobody saying a word about it. The net result was that the longer I was in it the more I favoured the British Army. I knew that, if I had to take my chances on the battlefield, I'd rather take them with the British than with anyone else in the world.

It was near Pembigon that I had a ringside seat at one of the last battles of the Burma Campaign. There was a broken railway bridge across the river that had been blown up in '42, but the framework was still there and it was possible to walk across the sleepers that were resting on the tracks. Corporal Rivers called me over and told me he'd been detailed to set up a forward observation post on the other side of the river. I and another private would go along with him. He said we'd go out around five o'clock after an early meal, while it was still light, so that we could survey the area and find a place to stay.

By half past five we'd crossed the river. We were a couple of hundred yards from the bank, about the same distance from a forward outpost, heavily wired and dug-in, facing the main path of the battalion. Our vantage point was underneath a Burmese house in which people were still living. What they thought about it I've never discovered, but we were settled in amongst the stilts on which the houses were raised because of the unpredictable influx of water.

It was my turn on guard, we were doing two hours on, two off, and I was thinking it's a nice quiet evening, when suddenly a machine gun opened up, one of ours, from the forward post, part of the river defences. Very lights went up, rockets went up, and the noise roared to a crescendo with hand grenades exploding and heavy machine guns firing non-stop. A Japanese party evidently launched as a suicide mission must have hit the wire. Further up the road, there would be a big contingent crossing and those hurled against the wire were expected to keep us engaged.

The gunfire died down, the rockets fizzled out and the Very lights faded; then the whole shebang started up all over again. Finally, the noise stuttered to a clattering halt with the odd obstinate rifle shot, a little burst from a Bren, a couple of inconsequential hand-grenades, then complete and utter silence.

It was a very long night, but the dawn came quickly and our Company Commander came over the bridge with a couple of sergeants looking for us. The Captain was glad to find us unharmed because we were in such an exposed position. Rivers told him we'd heard a lot and seen a lot in the sky but nothing on the ground. Apparently, we'd sat out comfortably a savage battle where dozens of Japanese had been blown to bits and the battalion was now following up the retiring enemy in strength.

A couple of days later, my familiar winged Dracula caught up with me, took his nip of Berkovitz blood, and I was on my back with malaria again. When I got out of hospital, the Border Regiment had moved on and, when I rejoined the Reivers, I found myself in the middle of a spate of rumours flying around the camp. The enemy was in headlong retreat, there was no doubt about that, but the conflicting stories were all to do with surrender, and some men swore it had already happened. The Germans had capitulated a couple of months before, on May $8^{th,}$ 1945, and the Japanese on their own against the rest of the world knew they hadn't a hope in hell of surviving for long.

When we were told to parade for a special announcement, we all knew what to expect; hostilities had ended in the East as well. An Intelligence Officer had come down from HQ to talk to us. He informed us that the war in Burma was almost over, as if we didn't know, but we still had another operation to undertake before we sewed the whole thing up: the invasion of Malaya. We were so close to Malaya, but it would be an enormous task to swing us round. He knew we had all done our time, but assured us it was solely logistical and geographical tactics that made moving into Malaya essential. After that we'd definitely go home. It didn't please us an awful lot, but being British soldiers, we said okay, we'd go into Malaya, and we only grumbled out of the sides of our mouths.

After the officer left, we had supper, and no sooner had we finished than we were called out on parade again. The RSM addressed us and relayed orders from above that we were to undertake some extra training. Extra training! This, for some blokes who'd slogged through two campaigns already! What more could we be taught about survival? As for me, I was nearly 40, riddled with dysentery and just about at the end of my tether. We'd all had malaria and the suppressive treatment we'd been getting through the anti-malaria pills was, on the whole, very beneficial, but the side effects were giving us jaundice. We were all becoming synthetic Japanese – turning yellow!

Luckily, the RSM interpreted the orders reasonably. We went on a couple of easy marches, cleaned our weapons in a leisurely manner and did some rifle drills. Several officers studied maps of Malaya and we even received some lectures about the terrain. Then the rumours started flying again. The war really was over. We had dropped a new type of bomb on Japan filled with an explosive a hundred times more powerful than any that were known. Hiroshima and Nagasaki had been wiped out. Millions were killed.

Naturally, I dismissed the rumours for the rubbish they didn't all turn out to be. Even so, the reality when it was confirmed, though much less destructive than the rumours, was to us miraculous enough. It meant we wouldn't bother with Malaya. The war was over and we'd be going home.

I only believed the war was over for sure when representatives of the Japanese forces in our area arrived to arrange their surrender. We set up a big tent in a paddy field where our Colonel would witness the signing of the instrument of surrender. A lieutenant chose half a dozen of the tallest, toughest looking men in the whole battalion for duty – myself amongst them. I would be on sentry duty at the time, and responsible for calling out the guard. "What happens then?" I asked the officer. "Do we present arms?"

"Correct!" he grinned. "How did you guess?"

"And fire a twenty-one-gun salute as well, right up their arses?" I said.

"No. Seriously," he said. "Just stand to attention and scowl. That'll shake the buggers up a bit."

A Major and three junior Japanese officers drove up in a staff car, with a white flag fluttering over the bonnet. The Lieutenant saluted as they got out and escorted them towards the tent. The Japanese Major was an arrogant little bastard. He strutted along, obviously convinced he was doing us a favour by surrendering and, although he and his colleagues looked like a quartet of bandy-legged, myopic shrimps passing through an avenue of King Kongs, he wasn't a bit intimidated. In perfect English and in a loud voice that the whole guard could hear, he addressed the Lieutenant.

"You understand, I only surrender because the Emperor ordered me to. I would much prefer to die." "That can still be arranged, Sir," replied our Lieutenant. "Sorry we haven't got any ritual swords for Hara-kiri, but if you fancy a bit of disembowelling, I dare say we can rustle up a kitchen knife from the cook house."

In the afternoon, we formed three sides of a square in a large paddy field, and the swaggering Major marched in at the head of his defeated troops. He didn't seem so cocky now, looking neither to right nor left, but remained defiant and, as far as he was concerned, still unconquered. He barked out an order and the soldiers halted. He saluted our Colonel and laid down his sword, then organised the stacking of the arms from other ranks. As each detachment marched in, the officers laid down their swords and supervised the disarming of their men. There were hundreds and hundreds of them and it seemed to go on for hours.

At six o'clock the following morning, as it was just getting light, I was awakened by a loud roar of voices and a noise like a lot of hissing serpents. I left my tent to catch what was happening and saw a company of Japanese lined up in the field with officers in front of them bansaying away to further orders and swearing, so I was told, eternal loyalty to the Emperor in Japan. It was very impressive. They obviously meant it and there's no doubt that, if they got the orders to start fighting again, they'd have resumed where they left off, with or without weapons. For the first time I felt a weeny bit sorry for them; they really were a very tough lot of soldiers and it was much to our credit to have subjugated them all.

I will never forget this strange spectacle, the place and the date of surrender. It was August 14th, seven years to the day since Bess and I were married in London.

Chapter 23

A month after the surrender, it was already well into September, and we were still stuck in this bend of the Sittang river. The lads were getting restive. We had got the Japanese busy repairing roads and bridges, constructing POW barracks, helping the Burmese rebuild their villages and harvesting rice. It was dawning on us that we might be staying on for much longer as a sort of Army of Occupation. We kept making representations to our officers via the RSM. We pointed out that all of us were long overdue for repatriation. What in hell was keeping us here? To be fair, the officers were as much in the dark as we were and obviously troubled in case matters got out of hand. Given the volatile situation at home, with a newly-elected left-wing government led by Clement Atlee ousting the old warrior Winston Churchill, anything could happen.

I had just returned with a party of prisoners of war (POWs) from a rice dump some four miles away, when the Company Commander sent for me. I wondered what he was after. He seemed much friendlier of late. Maybe he realised I'd been at all times a dedicated soldier and perhaps he felt he'd been a bit too hard on me over the Bren gun incident. I had a feeling that, if the war had gone on just a little while longer, he'd have given me back my stripes. What he had to say shook me.

"Get your kit together, Berkovitz." The Captain told me. "You're going to Rangoon."

"Yes, Sir," I said. "May I ask why?"

"To celebrate your New Year with the local Jewish community." He smiled at my surprise. "We're laying on a truck specially for you."

"For me?"

"For you, a Royal Army Medical Corps officer and six privates from other companies in the battalion. They're all Jewish. Northerners. They're going with you."

I saluted smartly. "Yes, Sir!"

"You'll take along extra rations," he added, "unless you prefer to live on rice like your hosts."

During my entire service career I never applied for leave on religious grounds and, to be honest, I'd forgotten about the Jewish New Year and Yom Kippur. But the Army didn't forget and that shouldn't have surprised me. When I was a kid, my grandmother, my Booba, took me to the Pavilion Theatre in the Whitechapel Road to see Morris Moscovitch in a popular Yiddish drama set in the Russian Pale of Settlement called 'Siz schwer zu sein a Yid,' roughly translated as 'It's hard to be a Jew.'

My very first Company Commander, an elderly Indian Regular Army Major took it up with me as soon as I arrived in Rawalpindi.

"I understand you're Jewish, Berkovitz," he said to me in the Company office.

"Yes Sir," I replied. "And I'm very proud to be a member of that ancient race."

He smiled. "Good for you, young man. In that case, as part of your acclimatisation programme, perhaps you would like a few days at Delhi? There's a synagogue there and quite a sizeable Jewish community. Perhaps you'd like to visit them?"

I explained to him that I was Jewish, but not an orthodox Jew, and that I regarded my Jewish affiliations as ethnic and cultural and I wasn't asking for preferential treatment. I wanted to be treated like all my comrades, like someone called Brown, not Berkovitz. As a matter of fact, if I'd got a pass for a couple of days in Delhi I'd have spent my time wandering round the historic sites, standing where Nicholson and his sappers blew in the Delhi gates, rather than attending services in some stuffy little synagogue. To this day, my personal involvement in synagogue services is minimal. The last time I went to *shul* was for my grandson Saul's Bar Mitzvah, (in 1980) and I probably won't be as personally involved again till he gets married – if I should live so long!

Being Jewish can, under certain circumstances, be an asset, but I didn't want favours from anyone. Not from the army, giving me leave under false pretences, or from my fellow-Jews offering hospitality in return for a religiosity that didn't exist. But I was sorely tried. With me, being hungry was synonymous with being alive, and being broke was more or less a chronic condition. Towards the end of the week, when my paltry pay would be spent and I found myself in a strange town, I'd take a chance on locating some sympathetic Jewish family and scrounging a meal. Being Jewish stood me in good stead this way during our first stopover in Durban, as it did later, on leaves in Bombay and even before, back home in Caister and Colchester.

In Civvy Street, Jewish communal bodies, like the Board of Guardians, aren't concerned as to whether you go to *shul* regularly or put phylacteries on your forehead and bind them round your arm when you pray every morning, or even if you pray at all. Your father doesn't count: as long as you had a Jewish mother, according to the *Halachic* Law, you're a Jew, and that's enough to qualify you even for Israeli citizenship. Certainly, it was enough for the Jewish Blind Society who, when I registered as a blind person in 1974, sent an official down to see me and without further ado enrolled me as a member, and thereafter posted me a small pension every month.

You certainly couldn't escape from your Jewishness in the East End, not that you wanted to. It invaded even the realms of sport. It must have been in the 'twenties, before my first trip to America when Hymie, my 'turf adviser,' urged me to put all my money on Rothschild's horse, Galleon's Reach, a rank outsider. The nag's form didn't seem to justify such recklessness, but Hymie's usual caution had been overcome by a feverish conviction on the part of everyone else in Bedford Street that Rothschild would provide a winner for Passover. Indeed, the horse came up trumps, winning at twenty to one, which netted me sixty pounds from my three pounds outlay. For years, thereafter, I leaned heavily on the Jewish connection around Easter time, but Rothschild didn't come up with any more pre-Passover goodies, and eventually I had to write him off reluctantly as another anti-Semite.

But while the Rothschild money lasted, I had a ball. In my whole life, I'd never had sixty-three pounds in my pocket before. I was living on my own in a seven-shillings per week furnished room in Bedford Street and, when I could afford it, had my meals at Bowlmer's, a little restaurant down the road. On Monday morning, I went in to Bowlmer's for breakfast and changed a pound. I went in on Tuesday morning for breakfast, same procedure, another pound. Mrs Bowlmer looked at me curiously. On Wednesday I changed yet another crisp new green Fisher: Mrs Bowlmer was getting very interested. When on Thursday I came in for breakfast and paid with a pound note, she couldn't hold back any longer and asked: "Sam, are you working?"

"Mrs Bowlmer," I said. "If I was working, could I afford to change a pound note every day for a week?"

The Burmese Jews gave us a lovely time in Rangoon. They wined and dined us lavishly with their own and our extra food, courtesy of India Command. They treated us like young English lords, who had dropped from the skies to rescue them. Maybe we deserved to be held in such affectionate respect. After all, hadn't we liberated them from the hated Japanese who, to be truthful, had maltreated them no worse than the rest of the population?

My fellow travellers were a pretty nice bunch but, apart from the accident of birth, I had very little in common with them. I had even less in common with my hosts, who were mainly of the merchant and shop-keeping class. They spoke no Yiddish and their liturgy was couched in a strange, Oriental accented Hebrew. Our sole means of communication was therefore a somewhat restricted English.

I made two brief, obligatory appearances in the dingy little synagogue, once on the Jewish New Year and again a week or so later for the Yom Kippur service, when my sins were ritually shriven for another year.

Most of my leave I spent on my own, enjoying myself walking around town and visiting the pagodas, monuments and other places of interest. The Shwedagon Pagoda so fascinated me, I could comfortably have spent my entire ten days there. A huge, elegant, bell-shaped structure with lots of gold-encrusted shrines around its base and gold leaf decorating the thrusting, handle-shaped spike, it was reputed to be more than 2,500 years old.

Apart from the synagogue visits and meals, I only met up with my fellow Borderers in the billets at bed-time or in the evening, when we'd got a whist, bridge or solo card school together. The doctor from the RAMC was a skilled player and two of the privates were expert at whist and reasonably proficient at bridge. I hadn't had a chance to play bridge for years, so I welcomed the opportunity of relaxing with this most intriguing of card games. It reminds me of the young man travelling in a first-class railway carriage in pre-Hitler Germany, hearing the door slam in another compartment and the raucous call: "Any Jews in here?" Finally, his own carriage door slid open and a close cropped blonde man poked his head in. "Any Jews in here?" The young man, a powerfully-built six foot two in his socks, rose belligerently to his feet. "Yes" he challenged. "I'm a Jew. What about it?"

"Come along with me" said the blonde head. "We need a fourth at bridge."

There was more excitement when I got back to camp. Hot and sticky, I stripped down to my shorts with the intention of having a dip in the river, when half a dozen of our men crowded into the tent. Sergeant White spoke first. "Sam, we want you to represent us." Before I could say anything, the others started talking all at once. I couldn't make head or tail of what they were trying to tell me. I held up my hand for them to pause: "Wait a minute, boys," I said. "You know I've been on leave. I don't know what you're talking about. Let old Chalky speak. Give him a chance – he is the senior soldier present." From what Sergeant White said, it emerged that the resentment over delays in repatriation that had been building up for weeks had come to a head with the news that the Minister of Defence was coming to Burma to ascertain at first hand the extent of our grievances. Someone was delegated to go to Rangoon to see him on behalf of the Regiment. So much was clear, and I was all for it. To be chosen as the 9th Battalion's spokesman was an undreamed-of honour. I couldn't for the life of me understand why I'd been picked. I'd never made any secret of my left wing affiliations, but neither had I attempted to foment unrest in respect of poor pay or onerous disciplinary conditions. I understood all about that when I volunteered for the army and I was determined to become a first-class soldier within those limitations. I had no axe to grind. I had no ideology to sell. I peddled no convictions, had no barrack-room law. The boys knew me, not as an agitator but as a reasonable bloke, a non-smoker (I always gave up my cigarette ration in return for chocolate, if any was going), a moderate drinker, easy about swapping fatigues and, being a strong swimmer, always ready to volunteer for Reiver Recces that took us across the River. As well, after that brush with the Japanese out in the elephant grass, I'd got the reputation of having a cool head in an emergency.

Accepting the job wasn't a simple yes or no situation. I wasn't the Colonel's first choice. For me, that complicated matters. It was a question of loyalties. The men had cribbed and insisted they had certain rights as Territorials, which legitimately entitled them to select me. I wasn't so sure about that. It smacked somewhat of a breach of discipline and, in a way, I rather resented them putting up my name without consulting me, though with the best possible intentions. Anyhow, I told them I was very honoured by their approach, but I must first have a few words with the Sergeant Major to make sure it was strictly by the book.

I went into the Company office, stood to attention, and announced myself. "Private Sam Berkovitz, Sir. Requesting short interview."

"All right," said the Sergeant Major. "Stand easy, Berkovitz. Now, what's on your mind?" "Quite a bit Sarn't Major. First of all, may I ask, is it true that the new Defence Minister is scheduled to pay us a visit in Rangoon?"

"Quite true. Next?" he replied

"Have I been nominated to speak to him on behalf of the entire Regiment? I said

"Also true. Should be on detail orders tomorrow morning."

"I can't believe it, Sir," I said.

"You can believe it," returned the Sergeant Major. "You have my word on it Private Berkovitz." "Another thing, Sir," I pressed. "Was the Colonel's original nomination someone else? And did the men object and ask for me?"

The Sergeant Major nodded. "Quite so. The Colonel's nomination was Sergeant Martin."

"Martin's a great bloke," I said. "He's young, smart, brave, intelligent. I'd have picked him myself." "I'm glad to hear you say that." The Sergeant Major seemed pleased. "Martin was my personal recommendation."

"But you overruled the Colonel's choice in my favour!" I shook my head. "I can't understand it! It's probably not legal according to King's Regs. anyway."

"Wrong!" The Sergeant Major was emphatic. "It's perfectly legal. Absolutely correct. The whole thing was conducted through the proper channels. Happy now, Berkovitz?"

"Well, Sir," I said. "I'm honoured to be picked by the men to represent them, but I can't honestly say I'm happy."

"You don't have to be happy." Returned the Sergeant Major. "So long as the men are happy."

"How can they be happy with me? I'm a comparative newcomer. Only the two other Fusiliers in this outfit have known me for any length of time. Martin's been part of the Regiment since you were Territorials. Besides, he's a Northerner, from Umbria like most of you blokes. I'm a foreigner from down south. A Jewish pants presser from Whitechapel."

The Sergeant Major cut me short. "I don't care if you're a head-hunter from Timbuktu! You're a good soldier, Sam. Almost too good to be true. A perfect service record." He gave a little grin.

"Except, if I can put it that way, for one teeny blot on your escutcheon."

"Oh that." I said. "It wasn't my fault. Everybody knows Wilkins lost the bloody Bren."

"Be that as it may, when you go to Rangoon you'll get your two stripes back and probably a third one to tack up for good measure. Sergeant Berkovitz, how does that sound?"

"Sounds alright." I still wasn't mollified. "But I don't want any stripes I haven't earned, Sarn't Major."

"The third's only Acting, Temporary, Unpaid. The other two you've well earned," he said. His voice took on a serious note. "The natives have become very restless."

I looked at him in surprise. "Not the Burmese," he amended. "Our lot. You must have noticed it yourself, before you went on leave. The lads aren't very happy about the Government's Python

Repatriation scheme. There's been a lot of murmuring. Deputations. A few more delays and broken promises and all it'll need is a tiny spark for there to be an almighty big explosion. The plain fact is that they're utterly browned off. They want to go home!"

"So do I," I replied.

"I don't blame you," he agreed. "I don't blame them either. After four years in India and Burma I want to go home myself. But just now we're stuck here, and you're elected Sweetheart of the Forces. They'll simmer down with you as their spokesman, otherwise there could be plenty trouble in the ranks. You wouldn't want that, would you, Berkovitz?" It seemed logical. I nodded agreement. "You'd help us all by going to Rangoon and speaking up for the lads. And you'll carry more authority when you represent the Regiment with three stripes on your sleeve," he concluded.

The Sergeant Major's arguments were unanswerable. He was a very shrewd operator, an intuitive psychologist and knew exactly what he was doing. First, he softened me up by appealing to my duty as a disciplined soldier. I'd been perturbed myself by the way men's tempers frayed so quickly in the constant debilitating heat; lifelong mates swapped punches at the slightest provocation. Secondly, there was the sweetly lobbed sop to my pride, reinstatement to my former rank, with an extra stripe to boot.

I resigned myself to my future role as Regimental spokesman and scanned the notice board anxiously for news of the Cabinet Minister's arrival, which would carry with it my automatic promotion.

A couple of days later, all bets were off. The Minister wasn't coming. We were leaving. Officially. All of us. We were packing up by the Sittang river right away and moving to Rangoon, where we would board the troopship, 'Duchess of Richmond', and sail for home. The news was sheer, unalloyed delight; not even tempered with the slightest tinge of regret that the Berkovitz promotion would once again be scrubbed before it became officially promulgated.

Chapter 24

We were swept up immediately in a whirlpool of activity. Before we knew it, we were loaded with our belongings on to the trucks of a light railway recently repaired by the Japanese and a small engine chugged us down to Rangoon in a matter of hours. There, wonder of wonders, the 'Duchess of Richmond' was already berthed, waiting to take us aboard.

We had a few days on the 'Duchess' while the 20,000-ton ship was being loaded with stores and taking on other departing units. We messed on board but spent much of our time in Rangoon which meant, for me, more pagodas as well as another round of farewells with those hospitable Burmese Jews who, just a few days ago, had treated me so handsomely. One of them took me to a film show in the Yacht Club, formerly a European-only enclave. It was the first Raymond Chandler movie I'd ever seen, with Dick Powell as the private eye Philip Marlow in 'Farewell my Lovely'.

I was being spoiled for movies. On our last night in camp the Colonel had celebrated by commandeering a passing Army Film Unit and drawing it into our area. The programme was Jack Benny in 'The Fifth Chair'. co-starring Fred Allen, his phoney feuding radio mate. Fred, someone I never missed on the air when I lived in New York, was possibly the most underrated comic of the day.

I would have liked to see more of Burma, but my four years of overseas service were spent mainly in India. In all, I only had about six months in Burma and most of that time was spent chasing the Japanese or on my back in hospital with malaria or dysentery. I came there, like most of the lads, predisposed to dislike the Burmese because of that early co-operation with the Japanese invaders, who had pushed us out of Burma in '42. But they co-operated with the British just as willingly when we came back, probably more so because we weren't in the habit, like the Japanese, of prodding their behinds with bayonets till they did what they were told. Personally, I didn't have much to do with the Burmese, but they seemed a pretty docile lot and, on the whole, rather good natured.

My young friend Tommy Dodd – he of the unsolicited twenty rupees – went into Burma with an infantry battalion. He was wounded, left for dead in the field, and posted missing by his unit. His parents received a War Office telegram reporting him missing, believed dead. Tom, however, was found by some Burmese tribesmen and carried off into the hills where they hid him in their village and tended his wounds until he was well enough to be smuggled through the Japanese lines into India, a week's hard slog. One up for humanity? Maybe, but, as the reward they expected and got was enough to keep the whole village going for months, cupidity could have entered into the equation as well.

The Burmese were Buddhists, which inclined me rather favourably towards them. Their religion wasn't dominated by a single almighty deity up in the clouds. Everybody and every living thing was a small part of their Godhead. When they worked out their life cycle through different reincarnations, they went beyond Nirvana and became part of the universal consciousness – or something like that. If I'm not more precise, you must remember that I'm only an ordinary working man trying to understand the world he lives in. I left school to go into the workshop at fourteen, so I had little formal education. I tried to make up for it by a lifetime of voracious reading with, on the way, some mainly untutored thinking.

In Burma, I was pushing forty. At forty, a man knows his own body: he's his own doctor, or a fool. At forty, he knows his own mind and has found his own road to Rome. Now, at nearly twice forty, the basic tenets of my faith haven't changed, except for a fanciful conception of God as a computer the size of a small planet, floating in space to the music of Don Giovanni.

I can't leave the topic of Burma without another word about the Prince Buddha. The country was full of his representation in all shapes and sizes; short, tall, fat, thin, sitting, standing, some of them with faces of an incredibly refined beauty, neither male nor female. I once bivouacked for the night with my back to some big stones. In the morning, they turned out to be the enormous feet of a huge reclining Buddha. Mentioning this much later to a senior ophthalmologist at Moorfields Hospital in London who discovered the extent of my blindness 35 years later, he told me he'd known that particular Buddha all his life.

India was something else. I arrived there as a card-carrying member of the Communist Party, full of preconceived ideas about the iniquities of Imperialism and prejudices about Britain's ruthless exploitation of the natives. By the time I left, I'd learned enough about this huge sub-continent to have nothing but admiration for the old British Raj. After such investigation as I was able to make, I concluded that Britain had established a very cheap, but efficient, administration. It introduced badly-needed hygienic practices to India, which certainly cut down the number of diseases. It planned and dug an enormous length of irrigation canals in the North and built a vast network of railways throughout the country. I realise, of course, that there was no room for that kind of foreign Raj any longer in the middle of the twentieth century but, in its time and place, it was at least as good and probably better than any other. Until the British, India was never united. There was never any central government. It was always at the mercy of invaders from the North, the Afghans, the Moghuls, the Persians and the Greeks. Into this vacuum stepped the British, close on a couple of centuries ago, but it might easily have been the French, the Russians or even the Chinese.

There is no doubt that, for a lot of British officials, serving in India was a cushy number with a nice pension at the end, but they didn't get it for nothing. They worked, and worked jolly hard, and being more or less of an independent outlook, they could bring to local problems a more effective judgement than the natives with family obligations or slanted parochial interests. The Military, no less than the Civil Services, weren't so hard-done-by, either. Until the outbreak of war, every British soldier in the Indian Army had the opportunity of four to six weeks leave in the hill stations. They left just a skeleton force below to serve until everyone had a period of relief in a more clement climate.

When the British came to India, it was just a mass of warring principalities. The history of seventeenth and eighteenth century India was nothing but wars; the Sikhs against the Punjabis, the Punjabis against Delhi, Delhi against the South, what we call the United Provinces against Bengal. Anyone who could muster a few thousand fighting men had to have his own little kingdom. It was a turbulent era and they treated each other far worse than the British ever did. They slaughtered near neighbours in masses. Historians speak about

India's golden past. Apart from countless precious artefacts, there never was a golden past in India. It's just a history of princes fighting each other to become bigger princes; for them the booty may have been golden, but for the people it was butchery, exploitation and crippling taxation.

The British brought peace to India. Under them there was no war for a hundred years. The maharajahs were allowed considerable latitude but could no longer do just as they pleased. They were tolerated only as long as the local custom and tradition accepted the personal rule of the prince. By building the railways and establishing a central administration, the British unified India and that is probably the greatest contribution any rulers ever made to the development of this vast country.

On one of my leaves in Bombay, back in '44, I was bored and went to a whist drive. When it was over, it was still a bit early to go home and, finding there was a lecture in the YMCA attached to the camp canteen, I thought I would like to hear what it was all about, and walked in. A young woman called Indira Gandhi got up and spoke on India's future. It was a quite interesting plea for independence, which, it was obvious to everyone, had to come after the war. She struck me as a vital, intelligent woman. I didn't disagree with anything she said, but what I recall most vividly about her was that she was such a nicely built girl. Most Indians are on the small side. Indira was quite rounded. The majority of Indian women seemed tiny, but must be fertile because they had a large number of children. I'm still baffled as to how so much can come out of so little; to me it's an incomprehensible phenomenon.

I never saw much of the family life of the ordinary Indian. On the march, if we passed through a Moslem village, the women would hide. Part of their faces were hidden anyway, but they'd pick up their clothes to cover their faces entirely so that they shouldn't be defiled by the gaze of an infidel.

The Hindu women were not bothered so much, and we could watch them freely as we went through their village. In the main, however, we made no contact at all with the rank and file Indians, which was just as well as there was no common forum of communication. We had no great understanding of, or sympathy with, their way of life, and to them we were the conquerors, their masters. We were the Sahibs.

I should say that at that time India must have been the most corrupt place on earth. The corruption was compounded by the fact that family obligations were held very strongly in India. If uncle Mothil got a job in the administration, immediately he had to find places for his three nephews, his four nieces, his eighteen cousins, his thirty-seven second cousins, down to the fifth generation. The result was that, with the family pressure on one side and the harshness of life on the other, no-one was going to miss the opportunity to get his hand in the till.

While corruption was a way of life in India it was, to a greater or lesser extent, a way of life everywhere. I would submit, however, from my own observation, that in India it was rife to the utmost degree. Everybody got a cut of anything that was going. We used to joke that you could tell an Indian the time and, if somebody else asked him, he would take ten minutes off first for his cut. It was the life of a thousand cuts. If anyone did anything for anyone, he wanted his little obligatory cut. I always had the feeling that, if I went into too big a restaurant and ordered something, by the time it reached me it would have disappeared.

If I knew little of the Indian people, I knew even less of their religion. I saw them burning their dead, which seemed an adequate way of disposing of them. They built up a nice fire, adding sandalwood, which has a pleasant smell, and put the corpse on top. Passing through Benares, I saw mourners throw ashes into the Ganges. Here, there were also bodies floating about in the river as well, but that was the custom and, if it suited them, it was good enough for me.

The Hindu has such a host of divinities and it's impossible for me to remember them all. Every week there was a celebration of some sort and you could frequently hear the sound of drums beating continuously, and probably not a day passes without a big religious festival for some special local deity. The Moslems we could understand as they revered Allah, the one and only true God, with the prophet Mahomed his Messenger. The Mahomedans comprised the bulk of the native army in India, along with the Sikhs who were not

Mahomedans but a Hindu offshoot. The Gurkhas are nearest in faith to the Hindus, although they look more Mongol than Indian but, of course, the Gurkhas are a special case. They have always been the most loyal of British soldiers and they held our utmost respect. When I was in Burma and saw the Gurkhas on sentry go, I knew I could sleep that night without worry. Any other night I kept one ear open for sound and movement, and always put a hand grenade on one side, my bayonet on the other, and at my head my rifle, in case we had to repel an attack in a hurry. When they were about, however, I dropped off to sleep without any qualms, confident they'd never let anything pass.

The monsoon was one of the things that impressed me most in India. I'd been there from August to about May without a drop of rain. Suddenly, towards the end of May, the clouds began to encroach on a perfectly blue sky. They built up steadily until the sky was black and then they broke and water came down in torrents. Torrents and torrents and torrents of rain. I enjoyed the colder temperature so much that I used to grab a bit of soap, run out in the middle of the paddy and let the blessed rain sluice down over my bare, parched skin. The rain was intermittent, but it went on for about six to eight weeks and brought life to the arid plains. Without the monsoon, India would simply disappear. Not only that, the monsoon has to be a full monsoon, which means there must be a rainfall sufficient to build up the water reserves in the chongs, the ghats and in the encasements built in order to catch it.

Some of the rivers with the overflow would be three miles wide, reduced again three months later to the normal couple of hundred yards width. But the water brought life. Everything turned green and the crops grew and flourished. So, whatever governments do, whatever people do, whatever plans are made, whatever things are plotted, everything revolves around the monsoon. In the four years I was there, it turned up fairly regularly, perhaps not functioning as copiously as it should have done, but always supplying enough water to keep the company going until the next rains.

We sailed out of Rangoon two days after our arrival at the port. Although there was a crowd of us on the rails, hardly anyone looked back. A lot of our boys had been left behind but, for most of us, it was with a feeling of relief that we turned our backs on Burma.

Despite my best efforts, my military career ended ignominiously and I was once more, and finally, Private Berkovitz, S. No. 13091795. In more than four years of active service, I had fired in anger just four live bullets. I killed or wounded none of the enemy. The only injuries I had inflicted in my war were on myself. I had stretched my powers of endurance to the limit and landed myself with incipient dysentery and recurring malaria that would trouble me for the rest of my life. For all that, it was a triumph. I had set myself up against fit young men half my age. What they had to do in the field I did also. I was accepted as a good mocker. To me, that was the supreme accolade, and their comradeship left me with an admiration for the British Army that will endure till the day I die.

Part 5

Back Home

Chapter 25

With Berkovitz's occupation as a soldier ended, it was back to *schneiderei* for me – making pants, the only thing I was good at, apart from martial arts. I don't know why I still persist in calling trousers pants. My professional association with the States ended more than fifty years ago, with my New York forays down Canal Street for the Shermans. I was now back in my flat in Cannon Street Road with a wife and child to support and I had to find a way of making a living fast.

Fortunately, there was an acute shortage of tailors in 1946 and trousers-makers were in demand. Ex-soldiers, fed up with rubbishy demob outfits, spent their discharge gratuities on decent new clothes. With my gratuity, I decided to invest in a workshop of my own. There was only one problem: finding suitable premises. As so often happens, luck played a big part in solving this dilemma. Chatting with a man over a beer in Dubovsky's pub, he told me of an empty little workshop in the yard of his house in Christian Street, which would be ideal for my purposes and he was prepared to let it for a pound a week.

I took him at his word and went over with him to view it. It was nearby, clean, dry and just the right size. The only snag was that it had no door. It had been blown off during the blitz and chopped up for firewood. Nevertheless, I gave him a month's rent in advance and sat down at home to make some hurried calculations. I had a couple of spare chairs in the flat that I could borrow and a second-hand sewing machine I'd bought for next to nothing years ago when a client I had worked for went broke. All I needed apart from these items and pressing irons, was a large table, which I could buy easily enough, and getting the electricity and gas supplies restored. The calculations stopped there. All my money was now accounted for, but that still did not include the missing door.

My lifelong friend, Hymie Olinsky, came and found me with my pencil in hand, clearly in a quandary. He asked what my trouble was, and I told him I needed at least ten pounds for a door with a solid lock. At once he offered to lend it to me, but I was reluctant to borrow any money from him right at the outset of my new career. Later, maybe, but I wanted to begin with a clean sheet, beholden to no-one, not even Hymie.

"You wouldn't happen to be going to the dog track tonight?" I asked him.

He nodded. "Yes, there is a meeting at Walthamstow."

I gave him two shillings. "Here's two shillings. Make me the first two number ones and number twos on the card." The first two number ones and twos romped home merrily and Hymie turned up next day with eleven pounds. If I'd bet on the third number one and number two I'd probably have made enough to open up a factory.

That was my ever-reliable Hymie. Throughout his life, Hymie only let me down once and, even then, through no fault of his own. During the war we were due to be in Durban at the same time and arranged to meet in the Jewish Ladies Services Club. I had already arrived, while his battalion was expected to dock in the area any moment. Unfortunately, our unit had orders to move in a rush. I knew he would try and contact me at the Club. I just had time to scribble a few words for him and pin it up on the notice board. It read simply: 'Hymie, wherever you are, send a hundred rupees wherever I am. Sam.' Some time later, I met a steward from the club who told me that the note had been taken down the same day by Army intelligence officers who were probably still trying to decode the mysterious message.

Back on home territory, Hymie and I resumed our peregrinations about London at the weekend, although they didn't take place as frequently as before. We always walked on Saturday or Sunday afternoons and occasionally of an evening. London was a totally different place now. We wandered through a deserted city so cratered with bomb sites that it was possible to walk right across it from Aldgate to West London without being obstructed by any buildings whatsoever.

Hymie had kept me going through three or four of the Depression years, when I was unemployed during the winter. Even when I married, I could always touch him for a pound or two to help me over a bad patch. There were never any questions, never any arguments. As a machinist, he was in regular employment and, though he was careful with his money, he saved it only to give to his friends.

Hymie was a wonderful chap in every way. He was quiet, unassuming, undemanding and remained a self-sufficient bachelor all his life. When he felt the need for a woman, he visited a pleasant, well-endowed, middle-aged widow who lived locally. She was a button-hole hand who had a small sideline in selective whoring. Hymie died in 1976. He was my dearest friend and, in my heart, I mourn him still.

With the proceeds of my latest betting coup at Walthamstow dog track, I got the door to my workshop fixed and had the electricity and gas installed. I slapped a coat of whitewash over all the interior walls and introduced a little heating. I had the windows repaired and, by the time I'd been there a year, the workshop was in a reasonable state of completion but, by the time I'd got it reasonable, I ceased to be a master tailor.

I particularly liked the workshop as it allowed me to be my own shop boy, which always gave me an excuse to run out of the workshop. After the early boom, we weren't making very much work. I did all the cutting myself and employed a good machinist, a finisher and a part-time presser. I had the opportunity of being able to gad about at all hours, telling my staff to inform any callers that I was out on business. My business was usually talking politics in Dubovsky's, or seriously engaged studying form in the betting office, which was cunningly concealed on the first floor of a dwelling house in nearby New Road. All in all, I was having a great time.

When the bottom finally fell out of the tailoring business, luck stepped in again. I met a chap in Aldgate who needed a small workshop. Carl was one of three brothers who were engaged in the renovation of Army and second-hand civilian clothing. He asked me how much I wanted for the workshop and I told him the first figure that came into my head, £250. He hummed and hawed a bit, but finally agreed to pay £200 for it, lock, stock and barrel. More than that, he gave me a regular job, as journeyman-tailor-cutter. I was now working as an employee in my own workshop, but I was earning as much as I had before, without any overheads or responsibilities, and was £200 to the good, the most successful business transaction of my life.

I worked for Carl and his brothers repairing Army clothing because all surplus Army uniforms were always slashed when they were sold, to ensure they couldn't be passed off as new. New civilian clothing could only be purchased on coupons, hence the demand for serviceable Army dress and renovated second-hand clothes which didn't require any coupons. This went on for about six months, when suddenly, as conditions improved, clothing went off coupons. It immediately took the shine off the workshop's existence and Carl was forced to close it down.

When I came home, I found the betting scene hadn't changed much. In fact, it didn't really alter to any extent until the introduction of the betting shops in the sixties.

There were a couple more Starting Price (SP) betting offices about but, even if you knew where to find them, you couldn't just pop in and place a cash bet. It all had to be done on the phone and you had to be a substantial citizen to have an account, which you settled up at the end of the week. I began to bet again regularly but, as a responsible married man, in small amounts. I still didn't smoke and had only the occasional pint of bitter so though, when employed, I earned more than the average working man, I spent considerably less on my little personal pleasures.

Backing horses remained a major industry in the East End during the garment workers' slack periods. Although street betting was illegal, the law on gambling was followed in the breach rather than the observance, like prohibition in New York, where nobody who fancied booze ever went short of a drink. During racing hours, there were queues of punters lining up at the entrance to little blind alleys like Cameron Place in Varden Street, where the bookmaker (bookie) and his runner stood taking bets.

The bookies were the aristocrats of the East End. A bookie would usually start as a messenger running bets and would work his way up through the hierarchy. He'd go round the workshops during his apprenticeship, picking up wagers. You could throw a bet out of the window to him as small as a shilling (sixpence each way) wrapped in a piece of paper carrying the details, and it was always good. It never failed to reach the bookie. You didn't have to worry. There was a high level of integrity amongst the runners because their living depended on it. If they were literate, they stood beside the bookie writing out bets for shaky old people and young ones and foreigners who couldn't read or write English themselves.

If you gave the bookie your own slip, he entered the bet in his ledger, pocketed the money and rammed the slip down in a big satchel which, from time to time, would be taken by a runner back to the SP office where all the betting slips had to be lodged before racing started.

The police, who got regular 'sweeteners,' didn't bother the bookies too much. Once in a while there'd be a pinch, which would be by arrangement between the police and the bookie, who would set up some seedy underling to take the rap for a consideration. The magistrate, dear old 'Dodger' Mullins (all Mullins' were 'Dodgers') at the Thames Police Court would always commend the police for their attempts to clean up this sordid betting business. Another magistrate, Mr. Humphries at Arbour Square, usually reinforced the automatic £10 fine with his own standard homily. His magistrate had a barrister son named Christmas, who was sometimes seen in the court and, in later years, became not only a legal luminary, but the number one British Buddhist. We 'corner boys' used to laugh at the way the bookies fooled the magistrates and carried on as usual, but I'm pretty sure those shrewd old birds on the bench knew precisely what was going on all the time.

Every now and again there would occur a strange phenomenon: a local tipster having a lucky streak, leading to a lot of winners. When the news got around that Tom Hall was on form, the money snowballed. I remember when Hall at the peak of his streak tipped 'Captain Cuttle' to win the Derby in 1922 and the John's Alley runner in a panic phoned his guv'nor at the SP office to ask whether he should continue taking bets. The guv'nor told him to keep on till post time because he was going to back the horse himself and was already funnelling the unusually high volume of cash through the 'blower' to the syndicate, which hedged his bets.

Betting for me was a hobby, a life-long interest and, as a person with very little money, it didn't matter much if I lost my limited stake anyway, because it wouldn't make the slightest difference whatever to my circumstances. For other people, it was an addiction, a drug, a disease.

Chapter 26

I had a distant relative on my mother's side nicknamed 'do-a-bomb-Harry.' Whenever we met on the dog track or at an SP office and I asked "How're you doing, Harry?" he'd reply "I done a bomb." I tried to argue with him regarding the pros and cons of how many 'bombs' one could do without exploding, but he wouldn't listen. By trade, he was a first-class ladies' machinist and could earn relatively big money for those days, up to £10 a week. On such wages you could have a servant and run a car if you were steady. But not Harry. As the years went by he lost everything: his family, who left him for his habit; his life insurance and every asset he possessed. He told me once that he'd flogged each single item of value he could lay his hands on, as he was a man of honour. Whatever he didn't do, he always met his gambling debts, because his word was better than his bond. If he struck a bet, he paid, regardless of the consequences. One day Harry decided to get smart and operate on the other side of the fence, so he started an SP office. He got himself a couple of phones, a little room, a writing pad and pencil, and set up for business. I know for a fact half a dozen East End millionaires all started that way with little hole-in-the-corner offices round the back of some old tenement with a couple of phones, and runners picking up spare cash from the workshops.

Well, Harry would get the reports coming in on the ticker tapes and start to figure out the odds: meantime he'd get a few bets from the punters, because the boys were sympathetic and threw a few shillings his way. Then he'd see the prices coming in from the Course and note that one of the handicapped horses, which opened at ten to one, was now nine to one, eight to one, thirteen to two, and finally settling down at six to one. Obviously, there was a lot of smart money going for it. That was too much for Harry. He'd plunge on it before the odds got any lower, and nine times out of ten it got beat. Still, whenever we met I'd ask him "How's the betting business going, Harry?" He'd grin and answer "I'm doing a bomb."

I'd say, "You were doing a bomb as a punter."

He'd say, "Well, now I'm doing a bomb as a bookie."

There was no hope for him. He died young, up to his ears in debt, a born loser. That was our 'doing-a-bomb' Harry.

The hard cases, those irretrievably hooked on betting, liked to regale themselves with the tale of Joe the Plunger. They kept on hoping that what had happened to him would happen to them, and they'd know when to stop. Joe backed the first winner at four to one, netted fifty shillings, backed the second at three to one and put the ten pounds on the third winner. He backed the fourth, fifth, sixth and seventh winners and found himself with £2,400! He shot the lot on the eighth race and his selection got beat. When Joe showed up later at the billiard hall the boys asked him "How'd it go, Joe? How did you do at West Ham tonight?"

Joe answered truthfully, "I backed all seven winners. But I plunged on the eighth and it got beat."

"Hard lines," the boys sympathised.

"Oh, I didn't do too bad," said Joe. "I only lost ten shillings."

Occasionally Hymie and I would pop into Sunshine's Club for a game of snooker and a chat with the boys. Most of them were former regulars, now a lot older but still not so much wiser. Even before the war, they'd been everywhere; some of them had been merchant seamen; there were usually a couple of ticket-of-leave men and one or two on remand. They all had tales to tell that had thrilled us as youngsters but wouldn't have cut much ice if they'd tried to peddle them now.

In the 'thirties, due to the few petty criminals who frequented Sunshine's, there was a theory that the police had a listening post there, as they had in most of the pubs in the area. We didn't take it seriously because it didn't concern us. Nevertheless, it was generally assumed that one of their spies lurked about the premises. Who it was nobody ever discovered but, whether through his intervention or good detective work, one or other of the boys would be sure to disappear from the scene for six months or a year. When he returned, he was welcomed back like the prodigal son and no-one thought any the worse of him. In fact, among his mates, a conviction was regarded almost as a badge of honour – a sort of status symbol.

Hymie and I in our youth listened avidly to their boasting, but made no attempt to join their shady clique. We were glad to work and pay our way and, even when we weren't working, we kept our noses clean. When, say, a shirt or some other desirable items of clothing turned up at bargain prices, however, it was very difficult to resist their purchase, even if we had an idea that if they didn't fall off the back of a lorry, they'd probably strayed from someone's stockroom.

It was raining so hard one Saturday afternoon that we decided not to go walking, but play billiards instead. Sunshine's was crowded. We had to sit while waiting for a table, squatting on an old pew stuck against a wall in the corner. We hadn't been there a couple of minutes saying 'Hello' and 'Been a long time' to all and sundry when old man Sunshine himself approached us with a tray laden with nosh. He emptied it on a small table in front of us, two steaming cups of coffee and a half-a-dozen of his *'spécialité de la maison'*, bagels so packed with smoked salmon it tufted out of the holes.

"For you, boys," he said.

"Wait a minute," I said. "We ain't ordered anything yet."

"I know," said Solly. "It's on the house." To say we were amazed would be putting it mildly. Old Sunshine was a nice enough bloke, but not noted for this generosity. In fact, you were lucky if Solly gave you a 'good morning'. It wasn't so unusual in the early days after the war for ex-soldiers to be treated to drinks by grateful non-combatants, but the goodwill lasted only until we started to compete with them for jobs. With Solly, however, no such considerations ever applied, before or after.

"Solly, you're a gentleman," I murmured.

"Granted," he said. "But this ain't my treat. You can thank Scruffy."

He waved his hand towards the bar where Scruffy Alec grinned across at us. A good-natured layabout of indeterminate age, nobody bothered with his second name and he was more often called Scruff than Alec at Sunshine's where, whenever he showed up, he acted as marker, part-time barman and washer-upper. But how could Scruff afford such a gesture? Solly must have been thinking the same as me.

"Don't worry about Scruff, he's loaded," he assured me. "Done a job for the bookie Izzy Richmond at Arbour Square yesterday. Never earned such easy money before in all his life. Ten quid for twenty minutes standing up in court and pleading guilty to running bets. And it ain't like being done for crime. It doesn't go on his record. It's only a civil offence. Now he's throwing Izzy's cash about like it's going out of fashion, so you boys may as well enjoy a bit of it before it's all gone. You two especially. Nothing is too good for our heroes."

"So long as someone else pays for it, eh Solly?" I said.

Old man Sunshine grinned and walked off. It took more than one mild jibe to insult him. Back in the bar our surrogate bookmaker whistled away cheerfully as he washed some dirty glasses. As for the 'heroes' tag, I thought Solly could have been joking about me, but Hymie was an authentic hero, wounded three times in action. Talk about that first world war song, 'The Only Yiddisher Scotsman in the Irish Fusiliers'. What price Private Hymie Olinsky of the 51st Highland Division? With his mob always in the thick of battle, he became more Scottish than the Scots. The first time after the war he spent a weekend at our flat and Bessie cooked some porridge at breakfast to make him feel at home, Hymie spurned the sugar and reached for the salt, sprinkling it on thick like a real Highland Laddie.

Scruffy had turned up at Sunshine's a long time ago, late one Saturday night. He was skint and had nowhere to sleep. I took the cap round. It was the normal thing for the billiard hall fraternity in the 'thirties to help where they could, blokes right down on their uppers. We all chipped in some coppers, collecting enough for him to book a room for a couple of nights at Rowton House in Fieldgate Street, a stone's throw away. For a shilling a night he got a bed with clean linen in a partitioned-off cubicle, with communal washing and sanitary facilities. Cheap as it was, it was three times as expensive as the 'fourpenny doss' at the Whitechapel end of Bedford Street where, Scruff told me, his father had lodged as an Irish immigrant in the 'nineties, sleeping seated on a wooden bench, his head resting on crossed forearms pressed against a stout hempen rope running chest high horizontally around the room.

Rowton House was another of those cheap, living accommodation projects for London's working people beloved by Victorian philanthropists and bearing their names, like the Rothschild Mansions Flats, Peabody Buildings and the Guinness Trust Tenements. The same Rowton House building, modernised, cleaned up and prettified is now called Tower House and fulfils much the same function in Fieldgate Street today, except that the cheapest bed for the night costs over £2.50, fifty times as much as Scruffy paid.

That was the last time Hymie and I went to Sunshine's. We'd grown. Feeling our slow way back to normality, even our leisure had to be spent among men who shared what we'd been through in the war. We decided to join the British Legion. The Maccabean Branch was in Philpot Street, almost opposite where I lived. It was reasonably spacious, had a couple of billiard tables and, at week-ends, there was always a bridge game going on as well as whist and poker. The Legion claimed to be nonpolitical, which suited Hymie, who was utterly apolitical, very well. But I was a committed Communist. I still gave automatically the Marxist response to every question, whereas Hymie explored all the other sides first and still didn't come up with an answer.

The Party didn't object to my joining the Legion; on the contrary, the St. George's Cell encouraged me to do so. It was part of our 'boring from within' tactics, the strategy of infiltrating into important, working-class organisations that culminated forty years later in the spectacle of half the trades unions in the country coming under Communist influence or control.

Chapter 27

I rarely walked down Aldgate East without dropping into Whitechapel Library, where so much of my youth had been spent upstairs in the reference room. Coming out one day, still on my demob leave, I met an old schoolmate, Archie Bloch, going in. We rubbed shoulders on the pavement and the first words he said were: "You know, I never got that £75 back, Sam." I'd last seen him two years before, in Delhi, and those were the first words he said to me.

I answered in London as I had in Delhi: "O.K. Archie, will you have cash, or take a cheque?" Archie knew very well I never had more than a few shillings in my pocket and I didn't have a bank account. I've never had a bank account in my life; I haven't got one yet.

The formalities completed, he asked about my family and I enquired after his parents. His father had died and, still a bachelor, Archie was living with his widowed mother in neighbouring Parfitt Street. He was short and wiry, with a small clipped moustache and spectacles, and a very precise way of speech. He had a watered-down cockney accent, like most other Stepney Borough Council employees. Actually, I didn't owe him anything, but he somehow regarded me as responsible for repaying a debt. To understand that, I must first tell you about the Stepney Rent Strikes in the early 'thirties.

The Rent Strike was the most successful of all the Communist Party's activities in the East End. Because of the need for people to live near their work, it was difficult to get a reasonably priced flat in Stepney. The result was that the tenements, in units of two or three rooms, were crowded with families. Most of the accommodation was not kept in any great state of repair by the landlords. Some of the passages had no lighting whatsoever. You'd climb up to a fourth-floor tenement and not find a single light the whole length of the passage. Some of the smaller houses still had open gas jets, with a metal plate on top to take the flame. None of the tenements, however, had lights outside the flats. The passages constituted public highways, but no landlord would think of putting on lights as that would cost them money. It must be admitted that the average rents were not very high, although they were high enough in relation to what the average worker earned.

In the Stepney Communist Party, we had a very tough activist named Tubby Rosen, and he became the lynchpin of an organisation we set up called The Tenants Defence League. We had help from a couple of local clergymen, one of whom, Father Groser, became a nationally-known figure as a prominent Christian socialist. There were also a number of middle-class businessmen, not necessarily do-gooders, but people who really were concerned about the horrible housing conditions of the East End and prepared to lend a hand. It was what we'd describe today as a 'Catch 22' situation. The average working man couldn't live like a civilised human being in his tiny flat, which he'd found with difficulty in the first place and, if he were offered a larger one, he wouldn't move because he couldn't afford it. Four or five people to a room was the norm. There were no small families in those days. In the tenements where I lived in Bedford Street, there was an average of twelve to fifteen children on each floor, apart from adults, with a few grandmothers and grandfathers thrown in as well. Families of seven or eight children were quite commonplace. When there was a public holiday and we'd all troop out into the streets, there could be a hundred kids skylarking about in Bedford Street alone.

Tubby Rosen organised the first successful Tenants Defence League Rent Strike at Paragon Mansions in Mile End, with the help of Phil Piratin, later Stepney's first Communist MP The tenants withheld their rents until their demands, formulated by Rosen and Piratin, calling for necessary repairs and cheaper rents, were met. Tubby had a rota of tough characters constantly on call in the tenements in case some outsiders wanted to start any funny business. It was successful. The landlord capitulated.

Next, Tubby went on to Bromehead Street where, armed with copies of the Housing Act and local Council byelaws, he discovered that, though there were several houses of different dimensions in the street, they were all being charged the same rent, based on a percentage of the rates of the largest houses. He insisted that the smaller houses should pay less rent and have an agreed rebate on the excess already paid.

In the following few months, the Tenants League won several big victories. In Malvern Street Mansions the members erected barricades and instructed the tenants to stop paying rent. Eventually, the landlord offered an acceptable compromise. In fact, it reached the point where, in some cases, Tubby Rosen would demand to see the landlord's accounts and assess how much profit he was making on the lettings.

It was a very successful operation. But one day it almost came to a full stop. Tubby met me in the street and said: "Sam, we need money. We're running two big Rent Strikes, in Chicksand Street and Mile End and we're right out of cash. We've got bills to pay for our office in Commercial Road, including money for gas, lights, phone and cleaning. We must have some money, fast."

"How much do you need?' I asked.

"At least fifty to a hundred pounds," he said.

I whistled. "That much! The Communist Party can't help you – we're not the Bank of England."

That's where Archie Bloch came in. He worked in the Housing Department of the local Borough Council. He did not earn a large salary, but it was a nice, steady job. Archie spoke a couple of foreign languages, had taken an external PhD at London University and really deserved something better. However, he was set in his ways and happy to stay put where no-one bothered him. A lucky win on the football pools of thirteen hundred pounds gave him that extra bit of ballast that kept Archie a contented man and something of a philosopher to match his degree. When he mentioned his win to me during a casual conversation and I'd congratulated him, he pooh-poohed its importance or value.

"In life, good health and peace of mind are all that matter," he impressed on me. "Money doesn't mean a thing, Sam."

In Tubby's hour of need, I thought of Archie, who'd been to school with Rosen as well.

"Remember little Archie Bloch?" I said to Tubby "Well, believe it or not, I've just discovered that he's won thirteen hundred pounds on the Pools. He's got no use for money, or so he says. Perhaps he won't mind giving us a bit of it. Get three or four of the lads together and let us pay a visit to our local philosopher."

Tubby, myself and a few other members of the Defence League went round to Parfitt Street on Sunday morning. We knocked at Archie's door. He was alone and let us in, a little dubiously. "Archie," I began. "We're a deputation from the Stepney Branch of the Communist Party. We'd like to have a little discussion with you." We followed him into the parlour and I introduced the group. "Look, Archie," I continued. "You work in the Housing Department of the Borough Council. You know what conditions are like down here."

He nodded. I continued. "You've heard of the activities of the Tenants Defence League under the aegis of the Communist Party?"

He nodded again. "Do you think they're doing good work?" I asked.

He said "Yes. Very good work indeed."

"You'd like that work to continue, wouldn't you?" I pressed.

"Yes," he said.

"Well, if you want it to continue you've got to do something for us." I turned to Tubby. "Take over."

Tubby Rosen was about medium height but massively built with big shoulders, tremendous arms and a pot belly that earned him his nickname.

"We're all agreed the Tenants Defence League is doing good work." Tubby said. "We're all agreed that it should carry on. Unfortunately, it may not be able to do so. We're hard pressed for money. We need in the region of a hundred pounds and we've no way of raising that sum anywhere. You must do something for us, Archie."

Ernie Spencer joined in. Spencer could shed real tears when the situation demanded.

"Archie," he added. "If you could only see the way the tenants suffer, it'd break your heart." And he began to cry softly.

Albert Ross was another big fellow. When he leaned over Archie, he practically intimidated him. Albert was never without his briefcase. Usually it held a cheese and pickle sandwich and a quart bottle of brown ale. This morning it was full of papers. He took out a sheaf of official looking documents, probably summonses for non-payment of bills, and waved them under Archie's nose. "I'll sign my house over to you as surety for the loan," he announced, and put them back in the briefcase, a bravura effort for someone who was always more than a month's rent behind for his furnished room.

Archie was terrorised, impressed and confounded. He protested he'd had so many calls on his cash that he had very little left. He couldn't possibly go to a hundred pounds, but he wrote out a cheque for £75 and gave it to Ross, who stuck it amongst his documents and shook him warmly by the hand.

Years later, in Delhi, on leave, I ran into Corporal Archie Bloch of the Pay Corps. I'd sweated more than three years and just managed one stripe while, by the appearance of Archie's pink knees, he'd only just arrived there and had two stripes already. He was living in H.Q. in Delhi and was even getting a Dhobi allowance, so that he could wear a smart uniform each day to impress the natives.

That £75 loan gave the Tenants League a new lease of life and it continued to make its presence felt. It pursued landlords until vital improvements were made, including putting lights in all the passages. Some rents were reduced and we worked out an equation by which the rents were governed by the rateable value of the property. A number of tenants even got refunds on rent that had been illegally over-charged. It was easily the most successful of the Communist Party operations in the locality and made a deep impression on the people of Stepney.

Of course, to be perfectly accurate, this wasn't the first time there had been Rent Strikes in Stepney. Major Atlee, as he then was (later Prime Minister Atlee), led a much earlier strike in this area and that too was highly successful. They had probably taken place in other districts as well, but only the Stepney Tenants Defence League pushed its aggressive tactics to the limit.

Chapter 28

Even before the war started, I was becoming disenchanted with the Party line and, during the Phoney War, I was even more disgruntled. A brief session as a door-to-door propagandist at a South London bye-election in 1940 was my last public appearance on behalf of the Party. The Labour Party fielded the official candidate, one who was acceptable to both sides. They weren't really fighting elections then, so the Labour candidate obtained Tory support. If the constituency had been overwhelmingly Tory, then there would have been an official, Labour-supported Tory candidate. However, this constituency being entirely working class, Labour put up the official candidate. The other candidates were the opposition parties, an anti-hanging candidate, Mrs. Violet Van Der Elst, and a Communist, anti-war candidate named Ted Bramley. The anti-hanging candidate was an eccentric millionaire; she had no other policy to offer the electorate. She used to visit the prison where a hanging was taking place, sit outside in her Rolls Royce until the official notice was posted on the gate, and then drive off.

I went around canvassing door-to-door and spoke to all sorts of people, finding their reactions very interesting. None of them seemed terribly bothered about what was happening. They all seemed a bit baffled by the lack of action, nothing war-like or violent was going on. However, there were shortages already and people were becoming a bit apprehensive about the future. Nobody could see for certain what would transpire. Against my better judgement, I had to argue the case for our antiwar, Communist candidate. Most of the people at whose doors I knocked were not that keen about the war anyway, but none of them was against a war under any circumstances. What baffled me was why I was there in the first place. I was all for the war and yet, there I stood mouthing platitudes about Imperialism and that it was not a worker's war. This reveals what conditioning can do. My sympathies leaned completely towards one no-nonsense working man who, when I knocked at his door, said he was all for the war, one hundred percent, and I had to admit I was, too.

But what could I do? I couldn't very well explain that I was a Party hack, hawking the Party line. Our candidate was overwhelmingly defeated. He came bottom of the poll and lost his deposit. He got fewer votes than that dotty lady, Mrs. Van der Elst, who never made a public appearance, never made any public speeches and only had an office where handbills against capital punishment were available on request.

My Communist activities ceased completely when I joined the army. On being demobbed, however, I resumed my Party membership. When war broke out, I was already morally committed to its support and became physically involved as a member of the armed forces. This was long before Harry Pollitt and the rest of the comrades recanted yet again after Hitler invaded Russia, and took up their original position about this being the most just war in history. All the time, conscious of these anomalies, I nevertheless decided to give the Party another chance. However, I was becoming more and more disillusioned and steadfastly refused to join in any but the most pressing mandatory activities. I had a genuine excuse now for not going door-to-door every Sunday morning in recruiting drives. I was a married man with a child, and occasionally obliged to work odd hours.

Even in the heady pre-war days of Rent Strikes and anti-Moseley agitation, I was a non-conformist with regard to our tight, interior organisation. If the branch had accepted a directive whereby it was committed to increase the membership by ten per cent in three months and only an eight per cent rise was achieved, extraneous conditions were never advanced as a cause. We always blamed ourselves. Members got up at Cell meetings one after the other and admitted they'd failed in their tasks. They rubbed it into themselves, fanatical in their desire to punish their weaknesses and expose their own guilt. This type of self-criticism didn't impress me greatly. It seemed very shoddy. However, that was currently the fashion among the faithful.

I never took the penitent's bench myself. I didn't consider myself inadequate or feel there were any serious shortcomings in my work. I did what I had to do without any great enthusiasm. This was more difficult for me than the others, who really believed in what they were doing. There was this strong streak of scepticism in my makeup, always visible to me just below the surface, which made me regard with some suspicion these leaders of revolution, the vanguard of the proletariat, among whom I was myself included. I couldn't help thinking, if these people are going to change society, who is going to change these people?

Nat Cohen and Joe Jacobs had done their utmost to get me more deeply involved in Party affairs. They'd even tried to make me a real rabble-rouser. They persuaded me to attend a speakers' course at Marx House run by Johnny Gollan, a wiry, little Scot in his twenties, then Secretary of the Young Communist League (later Secretary General of the Communist Party of Great Britain). I liked Johnny. He was a shrewd lad, a clever speaker and a good teacher. In six lessons he taught us how to enunciate our words clearly, how to project our voices, how to gather a crowd, how to capture their attention by hitting them right away with something vital they couldn't ignore and then work in items of topical and local interest. He showed us the way to deal with hecklers and the use of stooges in the crowd to arouse and sustain controversy.

I learned to project my voice so that I could be heard above the traffic at a hundred paces past a busy street corner. But to be a really effective speaker, not necessarily a Pollitt, a Bramley or even a Gollan, you had to believe. You had to burn. I myself didn't burn, so how could I ignite others?

Gollan was probably the biggest beneficiary of the course. He didn't have a decent pair of trousers. I had an odd length of cloth lying about so I knocked it up in the workshop and presented teacher with a made-to-measure pair of pants with my compliments. This was welcomed, as the money the Party paid Gollan as a full-time agent was just about enough for his bed and board.

About as high as I ever got in the pre-war Party hierarchy was when I became, much against my will, a minor functionary in charge of Agit-Prop, a couple of cut-down nouns linked in the Russian manner, meaning Agitation and Propaganda. I distributed Party literature at meetings, which I arranged, and sometimes spoke at myself, usually to introduce the main speaker and move a vote of thanks.

Chapter 29

Although a place full of poverty, Stepney was not short of culture and people searching for it. One of the meeting places for my Agit-Prop group was Fred's Café in Maningtree Street, near Gardiners Corner. I used to look in on a disused warehouse next door, where the newly formed Rebel Players were rehearsing. Under the direction of André Van Ghyseghem, a highly regarded professional actor, the Rebel Players later moved to King's Cross, where we helped them rebuild an old chapel that they took over and renamed Unity Theatre. Tommy Thomas and the Workers Theatre Movement (WTM) had their base there. They were largely into Agit-Prop and I occasionally travelled with the WTM when they would drive a flat lorry to some housing estate and, using the vehicle as a stage, would put on a Rent Strike play, with the tenants gathered around in the streets forming a highly enthusiastic audience.

When Unity really began to function, it became a place where great talents like Alfie Bass, Vida Hope and Geoff Parsons learned their trade. It soon blossomed into a centre of cultural activity, pioneering the production of plays like 'Waiting for Lefty.' At the first performance of this Clifford Odets play, I sat next to a portly H.G. Wells, and was surprised by his high, thin voice, squeaking along with a final exhortation 'Strike! Strike!' like an agitated mouse. Actors with international reputations, such as Paul Robeson in 1939, were delighted to make guest appearances here in American plays like 'Plant in the Sun' by Ben Bengal, dealing with trade unionism. Unity triggered off a string of other small experimental play-houses all over London.

Around the same time, though not directly connected with Unity, a continuous efflorescence kept throwing up dozens of brilliant young East End artists. Names like David Bromberg, Archie Ziegler, Michael Goldberg, Harry Blacker and Ian Oskotsky were increasingly being mentioned in the posh Arts journals. Pearl Binder, now Lady Elwyn Jones, was one of them, much admired even then for her marvellous lithographs of East End life. She lived on the site of an old fairground behind Toynbee Hall.

Barnet Freedman's brother sold fruit off a barrow in Watney Street market. Barnet himself, an artist born in Stepney, sold his canvases to national collections like the Tate. He married an Italian Contessa and eventually was recognised as a great teacher and brilliant portrait painter. Freedman's talisman was an old waistcoat, which he always wore while painting. It looked as though it belonged to the first long-pants suit he'd had for his Bar Mitzvah. As he grew older and fatter, he had extra pieces of cloth sewn in until, when he died, there were more patches in his waistcoat than original material.

Also blooming in the East End's artistic flowering were any number of youthful musicians and writers, even a few very good ones. Pianist Solomon Kutner became simply Solomon and recorded Chopin etudes like an angel. He had, in common with Hymie and me, a love of horseracing and the Holborn Empire.

Young Giovanni Barbirolli studied at the Royal Academy and played cello in the orchestra pit of the Rivoli Theatre in Whitechapel Road. This was one of London's earliest super cinemas, managed in its opening phase by Walter Wanger, afterwards a big Hollywood producer who was involved in a marital shooting scandal. Giovanni was anglicised into John, and Barbirolli moved to Manchester to become conductor of the Hallé Orchestra.

Those of us who wanted to listen to live serious music always had our free Branch 10 concerts at the Workers' Circle in Alie Street, where I first learned to appreciate the classics, or at the People's Palace in Mile End Road, or could traipse up West to the South Place Ethical Society on Sundays. For the literary-minded, the favourite was a walk across the river to the Bermondsey Bookshop, run as a hobby by a chunky little city magnate named Sidney Guttman. He was related by marriage to Basil Q. Henriques, warden of the Bernard Baron St. George's Jewish Settlement Club. Guttman had a wonderful voice, which he exercised by reading us short stories and snippets from the classics when he ran out of the West End theatrical and literary celebrities he usually managed to entice down to talk to us.

One of my oldest and closest friends, Simon Blumenfeld, wrote a very influential novel in 1935, still admired today, about the lives of ordinary Jewish people in the East End It was entitled, provocatively, 'Jew Boy'. I appeared in this novel as a character who leaves the East End to visit America. It even describes the identical method I used to smuggle my way into America from Canada, which I related to Simon on my return to Stepney. Simon set the tradition for a succession of Jewish writers such as Kops, Mankowitz and Wesker.

Of course, any extraneous activities in these areas weren't allowed to interfere with my serious Party work. At our regular monthly branch meetings, I rendered full details of our Agit-Prop successes and, naturally enough, failures, although without any of the accompanying breast beating. I usually managed to report that I'd sold my quota of the 'Daily Worker' newspaper, along with various books and pamphlets. I always bought a couple of these books myself, not to read but to keep up the sales turnover and gave them away or, if no-one would have them, dumped them in some convenient dustbin.

I had one constant gripe at Cell meetings concerning the editorial content of the 'Daily Worker.' We didn't have a decent greyhound tipster. Our horse tipster was first-class and had a better record than most of the tipsters on the big national dailies. A number of people in the workshops where I sold my 'Workers' told me they only bought the paper for his tips. The long, dreary articles we ran by Radek, Bukharin or Zinoviev were no doubt of tremendous interest to Nat Cohen, but I complained they didn't mean a thing to my workshop customers. Give them a good dogs man and more sporting features and we could up our sales by fifty per cent. I wanted these opinions relayed to the Editorial Board, but Nat was convinced I must be joking. I was never more serious about anything in my life.

The party-political scene in the East End after the war was a whole new ball game. With the defeat of Fascism at home and abroad, a lot of the 'thirties impetus had gone out of the progressive movement. There seemed no new focal point to engage the attention of activists in the late 'forties and early 'fifties. Phil Piratin had been elected MP for Whitechapel in 1945, the first ever Communist member for this constituency, and the last. After the Atlee government had run its course, Piratin was defeated when he stood for re-election and served only the one term. Phil, employed in the fur trade, had been swept into Parliament on a tide of euphoria after the defeat of Hitler, swollen by the votes of those East Enders who remembered with gratitude his and Tubby's Rent Strike successes and Phil's part with Joe Jacobs in the organisation of Moseley's October 4th defeat. As far as the branch was concerned, there was little change. Joe, who'd served throughout the war in the Ordnance Corps with his one glass eye, was back and Sarah Wesker, aunt of the playwright Arnold, a formidable lady, previously our treasurer, was assuming a more dominant role in our discussions.

Nat Cohen, his bullet-shattered knee making him a non-combatant in the second World War, had been bombed out and moved from Stepney with his wife Ramona and their kids to Wimbledon. Here, he joined the local branch of the Party. However, he couldn't stay away from the East End. That's where Joe and I were and most of his friends. He appointed himself a sort of Emeritus Professor of advanced Stalinism and was always in Fred's Café, giving whoever would listen little lectures, and sometimes big ones, on the theory and practise of Communism as interpreted and annotated by Stalin. Nat was never without a copy of Stalin's latest political pamphlet and always carried in his pocket one of his books that had a question and answer type catechism like the Little Red Book of the later Chairman Mao.

For Nat, Stalin could do no wrong. If, before the war, Stalin was the world's greatest thinker and educationist, Nat was now prepared to accept a whole new chapter of the Stalinist hagiography and acknowledged the apotheosis of Russia's Holy Father as the Generalissimo, the Field Marshal, the Mighty Conqueror, the Hero of Stalingrad, the Sole Architect of Victory. I would hear Nat laying down the gospel according to Saint Joseph to some new eager young acolytes, who would listen with open ears, mirroring his own adoration of the Master in the awed respect of their eyes. Once I drew him aside. "What are you doing to these kids?" I protested. "They'll end up Stalinist zombies like the rest of the Party."

"Schmuck!" he retorted rudely. "It'll be something if they don't end up irresponsible anarchists like you."

I was hauled before Piratin for breaches of discipline on several occasions and was constantly being reprimanded by Nat or Sarah for my more outrageous, off-the-cuff remarks. So it went on, my dissatisfaction and rebelliousness growing more vocal all the while, until my resentment at the way the Party was going came to a head in 1952 with the Doctors' Plot. Just before Easter, I heard that six Jewish doctors had been arrested and accused of attempting to poison Stalin, as well as a number of other crimes against the State. It was the Thursday before Good Friday when I read this, and I got hold of Nat that night and kicked up a row.

"This is a diabolical outrage!" I shouted.

"Why?" he asked serenely. "The Daily Worker reported it in detail. I can show you chapter and verse. They all made confessions."

"Stalin's set up a factory producing confessions." I said. "It makes chair legs to ram up backsides and induce such confessions."

Nat dismissed this as of no account. "Don't talk like a big putz," he said. "Their confessions were voluntary. They were properly witnessed and published in the 'Daily Worker'. Without question they're guilty."

"Well," I replied. "I've got no hotline to Moscow, I've got no hotline to Washington, I've got no hotline to the Quai D'Orsay, the CIA, MI5, 6 or 7, but it's obvious to me they're not guilty."

"Huh!" Nat grunted. "On what facts do you base that assumption?"

"Well, for a start, the wording of the accusations is preposterous. These same things have been said so often, they have become ridiculous. The indictments were similar in Czechoslovakia, the same in Rumania. Comrades get promoted because of their work and effort, Imprecor magazine is full of praise for their good deeds, and then a year or so later – boom! They're executed, and it's suddenly announced that all the time they've been agents of Great Universal Stores or ITT, or Redmond's Road Talmud Torah. I say they're patently not guilty. I'm prepared to put my money where my mouth is. Look, here's a fiver. It's all the cash I've got in the world. I'll bet you that five pounds they're not guilty. Now put up or shut up." Nat looked at me. "This is no way to carry on a political discussion," he said coldly, walking off. "I've better things to do with my money than to make stupid bets," he threw back over his shoulder. A few days later, Stalin died and within a week the doctors were released.

When I next met Nat, I couldn't help taunting him: "Well, what price six doctors? It made me mad when you didn't put your money where your mouth was. What makes me madder is that it would've been the first decent winning bet I've had this year. Wish I was as good a judge of horses as I am of human beings. I can tell a two-legged stinker a mile off in the city, but I can't judge a four-legged one when he's lined up in front of my nose on the racetrack."

Gradually, I dropped out of all Party activities. As far as I know, I wasn't officially expelled and I didn't resign. I just eased myself out and I, and apparently they, couldn't have cared less.

Nat had actually been chucked out of the Party once. He'd disagreed openly with the interpretation of some Moscow-inspired directive. Nat was proved right and the Party later admitted it was wrong, but it took a long time and several abject appeals before Nat was grudgingly reinstated. He never strayed from the Party line again, whatever it was, in word or deed. Joe Jacobs, also increasingly disenchanted, followed his guru, Nat, out of the Party. Joe stayed out and never applied for readmission.

A little after the Doctors' Plot, with the Korean war in progress, Nat disappeared on one of his mysterious jaunts, and was away much longer than I ever remembered before. When he got back to London, he was very cagey about where he'd been. After a time, however, it leaked out that he'd gone on a mission to North Korea with a local Party member, Mike Nabarro. It appeared they'd been sent to Korea to lecture to American and Commonwealth prisoners of war on the errors of their Capitalist ways. Nat admitted that they were very disappointed by the lack of converts, even though they'd been empowered to offer considerable inducements like 'trusty' status and extra rations.

I reckon those high-powered theorists of the Comintern, or the Central Committee in London, or whoever was responsible for sending out Mike and Nat, needed their brains examining. Both men were admittedly expert in expounding Party policy. Nat, the acknowledged elder statesman, always spoke as if he had a private line to the Kremlin and Mike was a brilliant debater with a legal background. In this Korean context, however, their appearance was against them. They were dark Semitic types, the sort the Nazi

Jew-baiter Streicher liked to caricature with grossly exaggerated features in 'Der Sturmer'. It would be most unlikely that they would be received as brothers by the cynical, battle-hardened regulars in captivity.

Mike didn't come back with Nat. We heard he'd fallen in love with, and married, a Korean girl and, after the war, went to live with her in China, where he became some sort of local official. In one of the innumerable U-turns of Chinese policy, however, he was accused of spying and flung into jail. They probably caught him smiling at something and, in China at that time, there was nothing to smile at, so the 'foreign devil' was probably up to no good, and promptly incarcerated. There he might have languished still if his relatives in London hadn't got up a petition and taken it to Downing Street, begging the kind, Tory government, successfully as it happened, to intercede on his behalf.

Mike, with his knowledge of history, wouldn't have been surprised at what happened. Revolutions throughout the ages have devoured their children. Danton was a God one month but, six months later, his head was under the guillotine. Tom Paine, the theorist of the French Revolution, would have rotted in jail after the storming of the Bastille if the American President hadn't pleaded for his release. All the founding fathers of the Russian Revolution got the chop. If Karl Marx had been alive in Stalin's day, he'd probably have ended up in the Lubyanka himself.

It is possible that Nat would have preferred that sort of spectacular finish rather than what did happen to him. Younger people edged him out of responsible positions in the Party as he aged and got less vigorous and more garrulous. To be truthful, Nat became a bit of a pest. At open meetings he'd raise points of order that should have taken five seconds and he'd make last five hours if the platform would let him.

Finally, even the youngest members ceased to pay any attention to him and that broke his hitherto indomitable spirit. He no longer travelled down to the East End and, when he died, his file still lay buried beneath a blitzed heap of Stepney rubble. The only other tangible evidence of Nat's existence as a lifelong Party stalwart was a posthumous medal from the German Democratic Republic for his services to the working class.

Chapter 30

My Cannon Street Road flat reminds some of my friends of what is arguably Hitchcock's greatest film 'The Thirty-Nine Steps'. It's on two floors, with twenty-two steps to reach the first floor and fifteen more to get to the second, thirty-seven in all: but what's a couple of steps between friends? When I moved into it in 1938, I rented three small rooms on the top floor. I took over the lower floor with three more rooms when the previous tenant, who also owned the adjacent garage, Mr Gorman, died soon after the war. I therefore had a spacious flat that even had its own bath, a most unusual feature in those days where virtually all my neighbours had to visit weekly the public baths in Betts Street. Of course, no one had a fridge or washing machine and chickens were brought home straight from the slaughterer's and had to be plucked and eviscerated at home. As I was a controlled tenant, the rent wasn't too high. It still isn't. Accommodation of this type in what an estate agent would call a more salubrious neighbourhood would cost three or four times as much.

The stairs didn't worry me. I keep telling my friends they don't have to commiserate with me for having to climb back up two flights of stairs whenever I went down to open the door for them. Running up and down the steps is a marvellous exercise whenever the weather keeps me housebound. Better than jogging, safer than walking, with no surly-sighted pedestrians shoving into me unapologetically or impatient motorists hooting 'hurry up!' at pedestrian crossings.

I'm an East End aboriginal. My wife Bessie and I are now (in the '90s) the sole surviving representatives of the Third Wave immigrants in this area. Not counting the Romans 2,000 years ago and the Normans 1,000 years ago, who were attracted to our shores and colonised Londinium, there were four distinct waves of immigrants in Stepney. First came the Huguenots, Protestants fleeing the pogroms of sixteenth century Catholic France, and bringing with them the fine art of weaving. They settled down around Brick Lane and Spitalfields. Second, the Irish, fleeing their famines in the nineteenth century, becoming navvies and taking root in Shadwell, Rotherhithe and St George's, to work as labourers in the docks. Third, the Jews, fleeing pogroms in Russia, Poland and Rumania, whose domain was the clothing trade and whose habitation was Whitechapel. Fourth, now at ebb tide, the Indians and Pakistanis, fleeing the third world's endemic hunger and poverty, who have replaced the Jewish presence and captured most of the *schmutter* business (garment trade). From where I live, on the West side of Cannon Street Road, right up to Commercial Road, there are Indian families occupying tenements and running businesses, Halal butchers, Pakistani bakers, greengrocers, cafes and restaurants, leaving us the sole non-Asians at this end of the street. About the only things these successive waves of newcomers had in common were that they could live squalid and work cheap and were usually exploited on arrival by their own, longer-established compatriots.

For all that, I like it here. I get on very well with my neighbours. Their presence reminds me that my own parents couldn't speak a word of English when they arrived in London more than eighty years ago, and also huddled together for reassurance and protection from a hostile environment.

As my eyesight has deteriorated so that I am virtually blind, Bessie does all the domestic chores, the shopping and cooking, and is my eyes when we're out visiting friends or on holiday together. She is also finding it difficult to negotiate the '37 steps'. I've applied for a more convenient flat but been turned down on the grounds that I'm being satisfactorily housed already and there are far more urgent cases on the housing list, which I can't deny. The Council, however, have promised to rehouse me when they tear the place down to make way for scheduled road widening. I've even had official letters warning me that this is liable to happen at any time. However, I've had these warnings before. For the past twenty years the Council have been talking about road widening schemes and, whenever they seem to be actually moving in that direction, some new economic crisis develops and they put back the old drains they'd started tearing out for the umpteenth time. I'd lay better than even money that, even if I live to be a hundred there'll be no road widening in Cannon Street Road.

We've had some very good years here, even while awaiting the Council's demolition. Bessie wanted better things for her son than I ever achieved, certainly not to end up as a trousers cutter. She encouraged and drove him on to study seriously at school. Passing the 11+ examination, he went on to the local grammar school, Central Foundation Boys' Grammar in Old Street. From there, he went to University and became a Dental Surgeon, taking up a teaching post at Bristol University in 1966. He became the first person in our family to get to University. He lived in Bristol for 21 years with his wife and two children and recently returned to London to take up another university teaching post. Barry's a chip off the old block. He loves to write – he's published a number of scientific research papers and text books, and he likes to talk.

My son's full name is Barry Kenneth Bradbury Berkovitz, an odd combination of Christian names. The Kenneth Bradbury middle section comes from an accidental meeting I had with a young man of that name, which resulted in an acquaintance that lasted less than 24 hours, yet left a memory that will endure as long as my family survives. I met Kenneth Bradbury in 1936, at the beginning of the Spanish Civil War, in Fred's Café in Manningtree Street. He was barely 16 at the time, tall, blond and softly-spoken, and had travelled down that day from Oldham. He came into the café very quietly, got himself a cup of tea and sat down at a table. Being a sociable type, I approached the lad.

"You're a stranger here, aren't you son? Where do you come from?" I asked.

"Oldham," he told me. "I missed my train and got in late. Someone from the Centre was supposed to meet me. I heard about this café from the comrades, so I took a bus here."

"You've come to the right place." I said. "Most of the local Party blokes hang out at Fred's. What's the trouble?"

"Well," he said. "I was due to meet up with a crowd at the Centre. We're off early in the morning to fight in Spain. I just missed them because I didn't pick up the train in Crewe."

I was amazed and impressed that someone so young could be so clearly driven by the ideal of fighting for a democratic cause. I willingly put him up for the night, gave him a good breakfast and took him along to the Centre in King Street, Covent Garden, where they already suspected he'd probably missed the train. I said goodbye and never saw him again. He was successfully smuggled into Spain and fought in the International Brigade. Untrained, the Republican fighters were no match for the professional soldiers that Franco had, together with backing of Hitler and Mussolini. Kenneth was initially injured in fighting but refused to return to England. He was killed during the defence of Teruel on January 20th, 1938. He was just 18. The following year, when my son was born, I named him Barry Kenneth Bradbury Berkovitz. I even put an announcement to that effect in the 'Daily Worker'.

Some time afterwards I got a letter from Kenneth's parents in Oldham, asking whether there was any connection with their son. I wrote and told them how much I'd been impressed by the boy, even after so brief an acquaintance, and so saddened at his loss that I was determined to keep his name alive.

When we first moved to Bishop Auckland in the early days of the Hitler war, I took my wife and Barry down to the Bradbury's in Oldham and spent the night with them. They had one daughter and Kenneth had been an only son, so they were delighted to meet his namesake, and, while he was young, they kept Barry well supplied with gifts of little, hand-knitted woollies.

Chapter 31

In the old Jewish days, the last shop on the West side of the street after Page Calnan's and right on the corner of Commercial Road, was just a hole in the wall. That's precisely what it was, a hole, measuring some six to seven feet in each direction, and that's why we all called it 'the hole in the wall.' Outside, it comprised a thick door with, at right angles to it, a heavy shutter secured by a solid iron bolt. The shutter covered the entire length of the shop and, when the bolt was released, the shutter opened out towards the pavement and became a sort of counter, where fruit could be displayed. There was nothing behind the shutter, no glass, no bricks or anything of the sort, just a view, illuminated by a single 25-watt bulb, of empty fruit cases stacked against the opposite wall, piled right up to the ceiling, leaving a narrow passageway between the boxes and a counter where a thin man could squeeze through.

The shop was run by the Cohens, two bachelor brothers, short, shabby blokes as alike as Tweedledum and Tweedledee and nicknamed the 'monkey boys'. They were about my age and lived together in the buildings round the corner, in a council flat. They worked a shift system, staying open all hours. The older brother was called Ruby, and he appeared to be the senior partner. At any rate, Ruby got up fairly early in the morning to do the buying in Spitalfields market, had his breakfast, sorted the fruit, set it out and opened the shop around midday. An hour or so later, Jackie, the younger brother, took over and stayed open the rest of the day, shutting up shop at three or four next morning, or whenever the trade allowed.

You might imagine in such a time, the hungry 'thirties, and at such a place, the heart of the East End, the stuff wouldn't be much cop. On the contrary, they sold only the very best fruit, even out of season and, if they didn't have what you wanted, they would order it for you. Naturally, under the circumstances, they charged a bit over the odds for their goods, but their early morning clients, long-distance lorry drivers *en route* to the docks, prostitutes, bandsmen returning from duty in the West End cabarets and clubs, and even the local police appreciated them being open at all, and didn't object to the slightly inflated prices.

The boys were born entrepreneurs, department store owners in embryo. In summer, additional to their main stock, they sold cold drinks; in winter, roasted chestnuts picked from a coke fire glowing in an upturned, old bucket with punched-in holes. They also sold cigarettes, which they weren't licensed to sell, and sometimes job lots of ties or socks. During the war, of course, when the Americans came, they could always be relied upon for the occasional pair of nylons.

Once, during Bess's pregnancy just before the war, she woke me up in the middle of the night with an insistent nudging in the ribs.

"What's up?" I asked her sleepily.

"Peaches, Sam," she said. "I'm just dying for a couple of big juicy peaches. Please!"

It was about three o'clock in the morning. If I'd lived in Mayfair, or anywhere else in London for that matter, I couldn't have done anything about it. Here, I just put a dressing gown over my pyjamas, shuffled in my slippers across the pavement to the top of the street and bought what she craved at the 'hole in the wall'. When I got there, I wasn't the only customer around, and when I left Jackie, he still was showing no signs of packing up for the night.

Some time in the 'sixties, the elder Cohen died. Jackie stayed on in the flat alone and ran the shop by himself. It didn't seem to make much difference; the hours of opening were much as before. He closed in the early hours, at three or four a.m. and, by seven, was trundling his barrow down Commercial Street to pick up any bargains that were going in Spitalfields market. Between then and opening up the hole in the wall at midday, he probably managed to snatch another hour or two's sleep. Jackie's trade started to drop off. He didn't appear to have as big a selection as when his brother did the buying, and the quality certainly wasn't quite as good, but his was the only shop open during the very anti-social hours so, of necessity, he still fulfilled a need.

Apart from not sleeping very much, Jackie didn't eat a lot either, and wasn't too particular as to how he dressed. During the winter, he always wore a dirty, old, dyed brown, Army greatcoat I'd got for him years previously when I had my workshop. Winter and summer, he was never without a flat cap, so begrimed with grease it shimmered with a patina like Cherry Blossom boot polish. When Jackie sold you something, he looked at you with his long, pinched nose, a piteous *nebbish* expression permanently on his face, and rummaged for so long deep in his pockets for the penny or two's change that you told him to keep the difference and were glad to get away.

In time, Jackie became quite a noted East End character. One of the glossy magazines running a colour series on picturesque East Enders, came down to talk to him. They were delighted with the feature and sent him a copy of the issue in which it appeared. Jackie wasn't so delighted. He didn't mind chatting with journalists, or having his picture taken, he said, but he objected to having it published. They were taking advantage of a poor ignorant old man who made his living on the pavement. It was an infringement of his privacy and he demanded compensation. After a bit of acrimonious correspondence, the magazine capitulated and sent him a cheque for £20, telling Jackie if he wanted any more he'd have to go to Court and sue them for it.

In the early hours of one Saturday morning, a couple of young layabouts pushed Jackie into his 'shop' and demanded money. He resisted and started shouting so he was beaten savagely about the head to silence him, until he finally fell to the ground. In a panic the men grabbed whatever they could lay their hands on. They couldn't clear out his till – he didn't have one – so they emptied his pockets and ran away. Someone living across the road had heard a loud argument and several screams, but didn't pay overmuch attention and observed a couple of men running away. Such sights and sounds were only too common in this area at that hour, so the man went back to sleep as things quietened down. Later in the morning, however, Jackie died of his wounds. The neighbour was able to give the police a fair picture of the assailants. They were picked up pretty quickly, and tried and convicted at the Old Bailey. When the police searched the hole in the wall, they found among the rabbit warren of old fruit boxes at the back of the shop some battered biscuit tins crammed with £145,000 worth of Treasury notes, including a roll of crisp white five pound notes that had ceased to be legal tender many years before.

Chapter 32

From 1951 to 1974 when I retired, I was in continuous employment for twenty-three years, twelve of them working as a trousers cutter/fixer for Julian. He was a good sort, more friend than boss, a most considerate employer. The 'girls' he employed, not one under sixty and a couple pushing seventy, were wonderful, going out of their way to cover up my increasing mistakes in reading work tickets or matching patterns. Most of all, I was pally with Rosie. She was, like me, a committed punter. One morning, I came into the workshop and found a big Upmann Havana cigar in its shining, tin foil cylinder, lying in the middle of my table. I guessed it was from Rosie. She knew I didn't smoke cigarettes, but occasionally enjoyed a good cigar. I looked at her and when she caught my eye, she winked.

"What's this?" I asked.

"What does it look like?" Rosie returned.

"For me?"

"For you."

"What for?" I said.

"That horse you gave me. It started at 10 to 1."

"I know," I said. "But it lost."

"It didn't. It won."

"Now stop taking the mickey, Rosie." I protested gently. "It came in fourth. I saw the board in the betting shop myself. It lost."

"You're right, Sam," she said. "And wrong. The first, second and third were all disqualified." If this extraordinary result isn't featured in the Guinness Book of Records, it ought to be. Nothing like it has happened on the turf this century as far as I've been able to trace. I'd given this tip to Rosie when she asked me what I fancied in the 4.30 race. I didn't like anything very much and didn't make a bet myself, but recommended this horse as having the best chance and, on my say-so, she backed it. I left for home at five o'clock and, as she was working overtime that night to finish off some specials, I promised to come back and let her know if the horse had won. I popped my head into the betting shop, looked at the board and saw, with a modicum of satisfaction I must admit, that the horse had come fourth. However, with my rapidly failing eyesight, I did not register a chalk notice that recorded an objection had been lodged, later upheld by the Stewards' enquiry. It appeared that, owing to inadequate course marking, the first horse had cut off a bend and the other two horses also took the wrong turning and were automatically disqualified, leaving the slow but virtuous non-straying fourth in command of the field.

Chalk marks were the least of the things I was missing. This was a year or so before I retired and the world was already closing in on me. At meals, I reached out for cups that weren't there and with my elbow pushed over the table plates that were. I tried my level best to keep all knowledge of my encroaching blindness from my wife, but Bess had marked my card long before I was absolutely certain blindness was inevitable myself.

I'd saved enough during my twenty-three years continuous employment for a couple of nostalgic holiday trips to New York, and Bess knew I was hungry to see San Francisco. She was also well aware I could no longer make it there on my own. She had a fear of flying and as she was not very mobile herself, she decided that I'd visit Rome and Paris instead, a much less arduous journey, while I was still able to see something. When, from her savings, she presented me with a week-end return air ticket to Rome, all hotel expenses paid, at Easter, she also told me I'd be seeing Paris as well, at Whitsun, but that would have to be the end of my journeyings.

I had to face up to the fact, too, that it would also be the end of my career in the workshop. Though I was delighted with the prospect of Rome and Paris, I pooh-poohed her fears about my having to stop work altogether but, even as I laughed at her, I knew she was right. I felt it in my bones, literally, as I nursed a badly bruised kneecap and a cut lip from a collision with a lamp-post, which had cost me a tooth as well. That sort of accident was happening to me more and more often. I was becoming a one-man disaster area, and I had the uneasy feeling Bess knew more than she let on, while underwriting my last sighted flings.

Rosie was more excited than I was when she heard about my trip to Rome. She was a devout Catholic. I remembered she'd once mentioned she'd lit a candle at St Mary and St Michael's church on behalf of Tubby Rosen, a Communist, when he was leading a rent strike before the war at the buildings where she lived. She said she'd give me money and that I must buy a candle for her in St Peter's Basilica in Rome and light it at the shrine of St Anthony of Padua, who helped the bereaved and deprived and was patron saint of the Little Brothers of the Poor. She had recently lost a valuable brooch and, after praying to St Anthony, she'd discovered a kid playing with the jewel in the gutter, where he'd found it when she left the church. She kept her promise of a donation for the Saint's Little Brothers and the candle would be an extra offering.

I told her jokingly she could buy a candle for me, too. As a born loser, I needed St Anthony's help much more than she did. "Maybe I should do that," she said, quite seriously, looking me straight in the eye. "Isn't there something you've lost you could pray to have restored?"

"Too late," I said. "It would take a miracle. My sight's too far gone, Rosie. No use me praying for miracles now."

"No-one's asking you to pray." She took two pound notes from her purse and put them in my hand.

"You just buy the candles. I'll do the praying. For both of us." Rosie told me how to recognise St Anthony. He was presented usually in a brown habit with a lily in his right hand, holding in the crook of his left arm an open Bible, with the infant Jesus sitting on it.

Thoroughly primed with Rosie's instructions, I set off for Rome on an Easter charter flight and booked in a few hours later at the International Hotel. I only used it for sleeping. All my food I had out and spent the rest of my time walking, taxi-ing and joining conducted coach tours. I hopped around the city from end to end, garnering in my mind's eye blurred, soft-focus images of historic monuments, like a demented squirrel gathering nuts.

First of all, of course, I went to Vatican City and executed satisfactorily Rosie's commission in St Peter's Basilica. Then, with the speed of an American tourist doing a round-Europe trip in three days, I saw the Sistine Chapel, the Coliseum, the Baths of Caracalla, the Forum, the Trevi fountain, the airy silver-grey elegance of the Piazza Navona and glimpsed the sumptuous villas behind the old tombstones along the Appian Way.

On the Sunday morning, I went to have a look at the Jewish quarter around Trastevere and visited the old Cenci Palace where Jews had lived for centuries. Someone who spoke a little English directed me to the main Synagogue, an undistinguished modern building, probably no more than sixty or seventy years old. It had been left untouched among the wilder excesses of Mussolini's thugs, and had been strangely overlooked during the Nazi occupation.

A wedding was in progress. Bright eyed, rosy-cheeked kids and adults dressed in their finest, watched and listened attentively, looking exactly like the synagogue-goers in Golders Green or Fifth Avenue Temple in New York. The service, floral and choral, was vaguely familiar except, when towards the end, the officiating cantor opened his arms and spread his praying shawl over his head to envelope completely the bride and groom, as if to bind them closer together to each other, to him, and in the sacrament of marriage, to the whole Jewish people and their God. I'd never seen this in a *shul* before. It hadn't happened at my wedding and didn't take place at my son's. It certainly wasn't part of the West European Ashkenazi tradition, so I put it down as probably an old Sephardi custom, peculiar to the descendants of the fifteenth century victims of the Inquisition.

In Paris, at Whitsun as in Rome, my thirst for history was unquenchable. I was like a miser grabbing greedily at visual treasures to hoard away for the dark days ahead. First, I deposited the now obligatory candle for Rosie at Notre Dame, just one, for by now Rosie could see even St Anthony couldn't do anything for me.

I was expected to go to the Rue des Rosiers if I wanted some good Jewish food, but I hadn't come to Paris for ethnic nosh. I could get just as good at Bloom's in Whitechapel and even better in my own home where Bess made blintzes to match Ratner's, and cheesecakes equal to Lindy's in New York. I had a half day's coach trip to the Palace of Versailles, took in the Eiffel Tower, Les Invalides, the Bastille, the Tuilleries, the Louvre and the imposing Arc de Triomphe. I wasn't fooled by the bas-reliefs on the walls of Napoleon's massive arch, those crossed swords, muskets, and soldiers with banners flying, marching to glory. Napoleon for me was just another Corsican gangster. Where his latter-day successors killed in their hundreds, Napoleon killed in his millions until, like Hitler, he got his comeuppance from the Russians. Napoleon created the very circumstances that destroyed him. He compounded all the follies of his predecessors. He got rid of the old dynasties and replaced them with new ones, mainly from his own family, which were even more brittle and more easily toppled than those he destroyed.

Chapter 33

It wasn't too long after returning from Paris that I had my moment of truth. In broad daylight I was unable to see my shears on the cutting table in front of my nose. Time, very evidently, to call it a day. That was in 1974. Now, nearly a decade later, I hear every week of another of my friends slipping away. I'm still alive, if not exactly flourishing. I only place tiny bets once a week and don't go to the pub at all, unless I've won a couple of shillings on the races or football. With Bess's pension and my own, and state help with the rent, we manage, digging into our meagre savings in the winter when the exorbitant gas and electric bills mount up. I hate to think of those poor old souls who've got to keep warm within their pensions, and have nothing put by to draw on when they need it most.

I suppose I should count my blessings. I'm still reasonably fit and can walk for miles. I not only can, I do. I know the whole area like the back of my hand. Every morning when the weather's fine, I walk across the Minories, past the Port of London Authority building to Tower Bridge, or take the opposite direction and walk down the highway to Shadwell Park, where I take a couple of turns across the grass and sit down on a bench facing the river, before I go home.

As a kid I used to see very old men in the little Ford Square Gardens behind Bedford Street, now an acre of dark grey cement. They seated themselves on park benches, looking straight ahead without saying anything to anybody, like I now sit here in Shadwell. What were they thinking? I wondered. Now I'm pushing eighty, I know. Nothing. They sit, those who can see, like me who can't, gazing into space, and that's all. Thank God I'm not deaf as well. That would be a major disaster, to be cut off aurally as well as visually from the world outside my flat, unable to hear the radio, no Mozart, no plays, without any racing commentaries, or my lovely grandkids ringing up from the West Country for a chat with Grandpa.

I've also become reconciled to the fact that there's no chance of my ever-seeing San Francisco, but I still hope to visit New York once again before I die. I won't be able to see very much, if at all. I just want to walk over Brooklyn Bridge and run my fingers across the railings, and remember.

Sam Berkovitz (left) and Simon Blumenfeld (right) in the grounds of Buckingham Palace attending the 'Not Forgotten' Garden Party 1977 for Disabled Ex-Service Men and Women.

Printed in Great Britain
by Amazon